A Rhetoric of Symbolic Identity

An Analysis of Spike Lee's *X and* Bamboozled

Gerald A. Powell, Jr.

University Press of America,® Inc.
Dallas · Lanham · Boulder · New York · Oxford

Copyright © 2004 by
University Press of America,® Inc.
4501 Forbes Boulevard
Suite 200
Lanham, Maryland 20706
UPA Acquisitions Department (301) 459-3366

PO Box 317
Oxford
OX2 9RU, UK

All rights reserved
Printed in the United States of America
British Library Cataloging in Publication Information Available

Library of Congress Control Number: 2004102465
ISBN 0-7618-2867-2 (paperback: alk. ppr.)

♾™ The paper used in this publication meets the minimum
requirements of American National Standard for Information
Sciences—Permanence of Paper for Printed Library Materials,
ANSI Z39.48—1984

The relentless efforts of Albert Camus, Fyodor Dostoyevsky, Jean-Paul Sartre, Hermann Hesse, Miguel de Unamuno, Ingmar Bergman, Richard Leland, and Terence Powers have allowed me to believe and accept myself in spite of my imperfections.

The hemlock pervades my veins.

Contents

Preface.. vii
Acknowledgments.. ix
I: Introduction.. 1
    Statement of Research Problem.. 6
    Research Questions... 6
    Justification for the Study... 7
    Justification for the Films... 8
    Aims of the Study... 9
    Outline of the Chapters... 9
II: Theoretical Framework and Methodology.................................... 11
    Complicity of Negative Difference... 11
    Cultural Contract Theory of Negotiation................................... 13
    Alienation.. 15
    Double-Consciousness.. 17
    Hermeneutical Ethos... 19
    Justification for Multiple Theories.. 21
    Methodology... 22
III: Literature Review... 23
    Literature Review of Black Cinema.. 23
    Rhetorical Texts Pertaining to the Content of Films.................. 24
        X.. 24
        Bamboozled.. 26
    Literature Review of Identity.. 28
IV: Analysis... 35
    Complicity of Negative Difference (*Bamboozled*).................... 35
        Africa.. 35
        Cultural Psychological Haven.. 37
        Socioeconomic Conditions... 39
    Complicity of Negative Difference (*X*)..................................... 43
        Africa.. 43
        Cultural Psychological Haven.. 46

  Socioeconomic Conditions...50
 Contract Theory—Analysis I (*Bamboozled*)...............................52
  Ready-to-Sign Cultural Contract (A)....................................53
  Ready-to-Sign Cultural Contract (B).....................................58
 Contract Theory—Analysis II (*X*)..61
  Quasi-Completed Cultural Contract......................................61
  Ready-to-Sign Cultural Contract (A)....................................64
   Symbolic-Linguistic..65
   Symbolic-Material...66
  Ready-to-Sign Cultural Contract (B)....................................67
   Identity Formation..67
   Assimilation..69
  Cocreated Cultural Contract..73

V: Analysis Questions...79
 Double-Consciousness..79
 Hermeneutical Ethos...82
 Alienation..85

VI: Overview..91
 Formation of Cultural Contracts...91
 Characters and the Contracts..92
 Breaching of Cultural Contracts...93
 Implications for the Future...94
 Researcher's Contribution...94

Glossary..97
References...99
About the Author...103

Preface

This study explores African-American identity through film, drawing from Spike Lee's cinematic production of *X* (1992) and *Bamboozled* (2000). The study brings attention to how African-American identity is negotiated in communicative interactions. In doing so, the study proposes an alternative rhetorical and cultural approach to the nuances of African-American identity.

Using contemporary theories from Ronald Jackson's (2002) "cultural contract", Mark McPhail's (1996b) "complicity of negative difference," Cornel West's (1993) "alienation," W.E.B. Du Bois' (1903) "double-consciousness," and Eric Watts' (2002) "hermeneutical ethos," the researcher explores the dynamics of human interaction: the manifestations of power, perception, and essentialist thinking and how these in turn penetrate through language in our understanding of others. Emerging from such issues are two questions: How do Ready-to-sign cultural contracts, Quasi-completed cultural contracts, and Cocreated cultural contracts impact black identity, in the films Bamboozled (2000) and X (1992)? What are the consequences for breaching contracts in the films *Bamboozled* (2000) and *X* (1992)?

Finally, this study makes critical arguments concerning the strategic positioning of language for purposes of understanding culture and difference. More important, it rearticulates black identity, making an argument for its complexities, which are other than historical and factual. It argues that black identity needs to be examined in terms of a more critical and culturally appropriate rhetoric.

Acknowledgments

So many people have contributed a hand for this moment. In no specific order, thanks to Jocelyn Y. S. Powell, Evelyn Stoleman, Lena Powell, Antoinette Roach, Amy Kopperude, and Drs. Richard L. Wright, Abhik Roy, Joseph Asike, David Woods, Richard Leland, Joseph Aschcroft, Paul Lippert, Pierre Rodgers, and George Thompson III.

I
Introduction

Film is rhetorical and functions as an epistemology. Like rhetoric, film uses analytic arguments, substantial arguments, and various other rhetorical strategies to communicate ideas; these rhetorical strategies focus on both film and rhetoric's function as epistemic. Film also seeks to explore relationships and provides meaning to those relationships. If these premises are the case, then film is rhetorical for its argumentative properties as a way of knowing.

Film also has the ability to blur the lines between what is perceivably fact and what is fiction. In other words, film can participate in the recreation of the "real" or it can make the imaginary seem real. In either case, the "real" or the "imaginary" is grounded in interpretation. Andre Bazin (1974) noted what he called "reproductive fallacy"—that is, the scenic, situational, character, oratorical, and visual qualities in film that bring about a psychological or emotional realism for viewers. The reproductive fallacy, therefore, is the blurring of idealism with realism.

Bazin (1974) examined the blurring of idealism and realism in the language of modality. "Modality" refers to how real the medium seems to be in relation to reality. Consider, for example, film. Film may recreate an event, such as a docudrama. Although the film is an interpretive and artistic creation, it may not adequately capture the true event. Nevertheless, audiences will perceive the artistic interpretation of the event as real. Therefore, the modality of the film, in this example, refers to its credibility and believability. Likewise, rhetoric may be perceived as more truthful than philosophy. In either case, both rhetoric and film address the issues of realism and idealism, thereby sharing similar argumentative and philosophical tenets. Rhetoric addresses the issues of idealism and realism by using critical methods and strategies. Rhetoric seeks to locate essentialist arguments, which are understood as truth-centered ideas. Mark McPhail (1996b) noted,

> Essentialism is a consequence of epistemological foundationism and posits a reality in which material and symbolic processes exist in and of themselves, in which they are justified either on the basis of some privileged foundational belief or on the basis of belief in some externally validated, reliably referenced "reality." It assumes an essential reality on the basis of which judgments can be verified or legitimized, and contributes to a linguistic praxis which emphasizes argumentation and critical discourse, precisely because such discourse is aimed at the discovery of essential truth. (p. 67)

Cinema has a dubious nature. Its crisis in representation and its rhetorical properties can be seen in the issues of satire and artistic license, which exploitation hides behind. The researcher uses blaxploitation film as a starting point to analyze this issue.

The blaxploitation films of the sixties and seventies demonstrate rhetorical properties that aid in the character development of ideas and images about black identity, which are seen in current black films. Blaxploitation films are films that exploit black people: "The films offer a warped view of black culture. These films contain the dreams and aspirations of American Blacks, and also sell the images back to them" (Koven, 2001, p. 7). These films disseminate essentialist logic and a language of negative indifference, which participate in symbolic representations of racism, sexism, and so forth (McPhail, 1996a).

To this end, black identity within film and the effect of an essentialist or adverse logic are of paramount concern to this study. If people are to engage in the interpretive process of understanding black identity and its relationship with cinema, they must first start with a definition of black identity, followed by a definition of symbolic representation.

"Black identity" is used to refer to people of African descent, their communicative system, and cultural interactions (Asante, 1998). Symbolic representation is a means for humans to express themselves and negotiate meaning in various communicative contexts. It is also the adaptation and use of particular sign and semantic systems, which combine for a unique and individual expression that people use to represent themselves intrapersonally and universally (Burke, 1966).

The association between black identity and cinema is one that aims to explore how blacks are identified, represented, and understood symbolically in film. The exploration into the epistemological function of symbols, their validity, and what they communicate is imperative because of their argumentative, iconistic, and ethical properties. Of central concern to this research then is misrepresentation. Although blaxploitation film depicts a time period, the same ideological misrepresentations still persist in Lee's *Bamboozled* (2000) and *X* (1992).

Symbols do not literally communicate what black identity is. Symbols only provide a language that communicates what something is thought to be. Symbols have limited access to the reality they represent. Within this context, symbols can exaggerate and embellish that which they represent, and such can be the case of essentialist representation of black identity in film. William Phillips (1985) reported,

> The power of film may be found in how it creates symbols for the viewer to identify with or use to interpret its messages. Film extends our ability to create and use symbols by making things, people, places, and events seem real. Because film is a visual medium, its symbols are frequently visual [thus impeding on our most intimate beliefs]. (p. 62)

Properties of cinema in this context are highly persuasive. Kenneth Burke (1966) warned that humans have a penchant to use symbols for both the positive and the negative. The negative is a discourse of difference. It is a way in which humans berate ideas while valorizing others. Popular and mainstream films use the negative to hyperbolize issues of black identity. Films such as *Coffy* (1973) and *Shaft* (1971) present blacks as sexually zealous, psychologically disturbed, and unrefined. These essentialist traits are just as relevant today because they resurface in contemporary black cinema.

Gary Crowdus and Dan Georakas (2001) reported that just because blacks are not dressing in blackface doesn't mean that Hollywood has abandoned essentialist discourse altogether. Essentialism is the understanding of an idea in terms of a singular reality. Moreover, essentialism is based on presuppositions and classifications that aim to debase one social experience while valorizing another. Today, Hollywood still makes a concerted effort to morph and conceal essentialist discourse within contemporary black film. McPhail (1994) noted, "[Essentialism] is an example of human symbolic and social interaction [and control], which has a number of rhetorical dimensions [and consequences]" (p. 4). One of these dimensions is identity—specifically, how identity is regulated and enforced through racist discourse.

Manthia Diawara (1993) reported that the impetus for the misrepresentation of black identity derives from whites' need to perpetuate their view of race. McPhail (1994) noted that the language of white racism permeates various social discourses. In film, whites attempt to define blacks through their own codes of understanding, and this definition makes way for misrepresentation. The repercussions of misrepresentation are staggering because black identities on the screen and off the screen become indistinguishable. As such, understanding the dynamics of essentialism and how it plays a ubiquitous role in people's daily perception and interpretation process is important to the communicative dimension of this study.

Haig Bosmajian (1983) reported, "The power which comes from naming and defining people has had positive as well as negative effects on entire populations.... The negative labels we attach to people and groups have effects on their identities and perhaps their survival" (p. 9). Both McPhail (1996a) and Bosmajian (1983) understand identity to be more than the sum of historical and biological facticity. Identity is both rhetorical and symbolic (Hall & Gay, 1996). If these arguments are the case, then black identity still needs exploration.

This study is rhetorical because it examines how language and symbols conjoin to form ideological representations of black identity. The study has an intercultural significance because it examines how ideological representations affect intraethnic and interethnic communication.

Today, black directors such as Spike Lee use cinema rhetorically and critically, transforming the social and political climate of a nation. Consider, for example, Lee's use of spatial narrative. Diawara (1993) stated, "Lee uses spatial narrative [as a critical technique to expose racism and prejudice] through hierarchical landscape of objects on the screen. Thus, space is related to power and powerlessness" (p. 11). Those who occupy the center of the screen are understood as more powerful. Lee uses spatial narration as a way of deconstructing Eurocentric discourse and providing an Afrocentric perspective. Two of Lee's films, *Bamboozled* (2000) and *X* (1992), are evidence of these rhetorical properties.

X (1992) is a docudrama, directed by Spike Lee, that is a reconstruction of significant parts of Malcolm X's life. The researcher will examine Lee's reconstruction of the historical Malcolm X. Lee's reconstruction also includes Harlem and central key figures in Malcolm's life.

Although *Bamboozled* (2000) is not a docudrama, Lee reconstructed blackface minstrelsy. Blackface minstrelsy was a performance style that usually consisted of several white male performers parodying the songs, dances, and speech patterns of southern blacks. Performers blackened their faces with burnt cork and dressed in rags as they played the banjo, the bone castanets, the fiddle, and the tambourine. They sang, danced, told culturally insensitive jokes, cross-dressed, and gave comical stump speeches (Mahar, 1998).

From the late 1820s to the early 1950s, blackface minstrelsy dominated American popular entertainment. Americans saw it on the stages of theaters and circuses, read about it in the popular novels of the nineteenth century, heard it over the radio, and viewed it on film and television (Mahar, 1998). Part of the researcher's analysis rests entirely on his ability to interpret what Lee envisioned blackface to be.

In addition, *Bamboozled* (2000) addresses social and political comments about race, identity negotiation, and politics through pivotal characters such as Pierre Delacroix, Cheeba, and Manray. Delacroix is a black television manager who works at a television broadcast agency. Delacroix's primary function is to create television situational comedies. Cheeba and Manray are black, without home and job, but are talented street performers. Their main function in the film *Bamboozled* is to work with Delacroix to put on a modern day minstrel show.

Although the characters and their situations are fictitious in *Bamboozled* (2000) and reconstructed from historical accounts in *X* (1992), Lee argued, in both films, that the identity issues with which the characters are faced are similar to the identity issues that African Americans face today. Blacks may not see themselves represented in blackface or as victims of blatant segregation, but they are always reminded of their blackness, what that communicates, and how it must be negotiated. Spike Lee communicated these important issues through character interaction; therefore, the researcher must be attentive to the dialogue that transpires. Lee used the narration and dialogue to communicate ideas concerning relationships, politics, religion, culture, and race and identity issues. The researcher's job is to examine the dialogue and narration to evaluate critically the culturally significant messages as they pertain to any issues of African-American sociocultural experiences. Lee examined black identity as a sociological subject, couched in assimilation and identity negotiation.

Ronald Jackson (2002) saw communicative and rhetorical conditions as cultural contracts that blacks enter and exit. This study applied contractual theory and the complicity of negative difference theory to central characters in the films. The study applied McPhail's (1996a) "complicity of negative difference," Cornel West's (1993) "alienation," W.E.B. Du Bois' (1903) "double-consciousness," and Eric Watts' (2002) "hermeneutical ethos" to explore advance issues concerning black identity. As such, these theoretical models provide a comprehensive understanding of black identity and negotiation. Moreover, by understanding the communicative and rhetorical conditions as cultural contracts, Lee's articulation of black identity becomes even clearer and more intelligible than ever.

The rhetorical prowess of Jackson's (2002) theory lies in the theory's descriptive and interpretive approach toward the negotiation of identity and the building process. Jackson (2002) submitted, "Identity negotiation refers to a conscious and mindful process of shifting one's worldview or cultural behaviors or both. During this process, cultural patterns of communicating and ways of seeing the world are at stake" (p. 49).

Mark McPhail (1996a) examined the relationship between language and identity building. The way humans understand one another is through language. Language is significant in humans' ability to make meaning and negotiate that meaning. Therefore, language is the ground from which humans establish opinions and ideas about each other. Furthermore, language is the foundation by which humans communicate their realities to one another. The rhetorical strength of McPhail's (1996a) theory is it's the theory's ability to examine the relationship between language and identity. Just as important, McPhail's (1996a) theory explores the various ways identity is negotiated.

Descriptively, identity is to be understood as the synthesis and management of social interactions affecting the collective self. It is also how a person can organize and arrange his or her collective self into a monolithic and presentable self. Because the self is shifting at all times, an individual must be cognizant that the presented self adapts to the current communicative contract.

Statement of Research Problem

The research problem focuses on Lee's vision of black identity as it presents itself for the researcher's analysis and of negotiation in Lee's films *Bamboozled* (2000) and *X* (1992). Of key importance to the research problem is what the presentation of these films communicates about the complicit nature of discourse and the construction of black identity and negotiation for African Americans. In order to address this issue, the researcher focuses his attention on three communicative dynamics: first, complicity with essentialist discourse and the formation of cultural contracts as they relate to black identity in the films; second, the characters entering into cultural contracts—how these have an impact on black identity; and third, characters breaching the contracts in the films. The second and third dynamics have a direct consequence to the examination of the characters of Malcolm X, Pierre Delacroix, Cheeba, and Manray.

The researcher realizes that there is a connection between the type of contract breached and the consequences that follow. While this may be the case, this connection is not a necessary focus of this specific research.

Research Questions

The present study examines the following specific research questions:
1. How do Ready-to-sign contracts, Quasi-completed cultural contracts, and Cocreated cultural contracts affect black identity in the films *Bamboozled* (2000) and *X* (1992)?

2. What are the consequences for breaching contracts in the films *Bamboozled* (2000) and *X* (1992)?

Justification for the Study

A population of blaxploitation films from the sixties and seventies functions on stereotypes (Koven, 2001, p. 10). J. Mikel Koven (2001) purported, "Blaxploitation films exploit individuals' desires to see black people, specifically African Americans, doing presumably what one expects or wants to see African Americans doing" (p. 7). Moreover, "White cinema, like western rhetorical discourse, looks much like a crystal palace inside with legions of residents, having accepted the inheritance of the subject position from which knowledge is universally contemplated, narcissistically discuss the world" (Diawara, 1993, p. 177).

This study recognizes that there are myriad values in black films that are often overlooked or just ignored. Both Diawara (1993) and Koven (2001) implicitly communicated an important idea. Whites have come to an understanding of black cinema through their own cultural lenses. Diawara (1993) stated, "The mode of representation of the nineteenth-century minstrel show typifies a principal characteristic...that persists in the increasingly liberalized regimes of later representation of a speculative self through the mask of the alien" (p. 183). According to McPhail (1996a), "Contemporary popular and academic commentators have criticized mainstream media for its negative depictions of African-Americans" (p. 127). Nathan Godfried (2002) stated that the "mass media further reinforce racism/sexism by changing history to suit the desired image of the dominant group and presenting stereotypic, negative images of nondominant groups, reinforcing the notion that in our society only the reality of a certain people is valid" (p. 9). Crowdus and Georakas (2001) expressed a need for scholars to direct their attention to the ideology composing black identity and not just its relationship to hegemonic interests. In support of Crowdus and Georakas' (2001) assertion, in *Bamboozled* (2000), Delacroix, checking over the revisions made to the minstrel show, is in awe when he sees that all of the black characters are stereotyped. In rage, he confronts Mr. Dunwitty, his boss, and explains that there is diversity in the black community.

Delacroix: These are black folks we are talking about.... We are not a monolithic group of people. We all don't think alike.

These previous arguments all are cogent, which suggests that this study is important and has value to the academic community and the public community at large. This study recognizes that blaxploitation ideology is still present in contemporary black cinema. The current study makes a concerted effort to identify this complicit discourse of essentialism and treat it appropriately.

The researcher has identified reasons for this study in the previous paragraphs and seeks to contribute to a new wave of discourse to rectify the problem of African-American misrepresentation in film. This study of *Bamboozled* (2000) and *X* (1992) can serve as a starting point to reexamine black identity and its negotiation.

Justification for the Films

Bamboozled (2000) and *X* (1992) are significant films and were chosen for specific reasons. In these films, Lee (1992) demonstrated his ability to bring together fragments of black identity and present them in an intelligible language. Both films are tools, providing insight into the areas of black identity. Lee's (1992) ability to carry out this daunting task was executed through dialogue, narration, the manipulation of the camera, the recreation of historical characters and geographical locations, and the signifying of artifacts, posturing as coded semantic messages.

Often reserved for speech, song, dance, and ritual, "signifying" communicates frequent statements, which have double or even multiple meanings. A statement, which sounds innocuous to a white audience, might carry a hidden meaning to African Americans (Gill, 1994). *Bamboozled* (2000) and *X* (1992) are no exception. Consider, for example, the use of slave ships, puppets, Mecca, and the American flag. These are all recurring motifs in *X* and *Bamboozled*, signifying myriad possible commentary about the politics of black identity. The explicit burning of the American flag receding to an X in the opening of *X* (1992) and the blatant use of blackface in *Bamboozled* (2000) serve as rhetorical strategies, asking the audience the question: Are racist commentaries a source of pain or a source for healing? These were ideological directions or misdirections made by Lee. (Although the researcher doesn't explore symbolic discourse of misdirection, symbols are important to mention because they contribute to Lee's motif as a film director). Ann Gill (1994) pointed out, "Signifying, then, is all of these forms of verbal misdirection. It is a mode of persuasive communication unique to the black community that involves various sophisticated rhetorical strategies that give multiple and metaphoric meaning to words" (p. 231).

Bamboozled (2000) and *X* (1992) explore identity through rhetoric, cultural studies, and philosophy. This study also has a rhetorical and intercultural impact toward the articulation of black identity; the study does this through Lee's use of symbols and dialogue.

Because of Lee's use of symbols and dialogue to communicate complex ideas, it is important to understand the significance of his strategy. This is an invaluable aspect to the successful analysis of both films. Burke (1966) noted that part of being human is the use of symbols. Individuals must not only examine the functionality of symbols but also understand the ideology aiding in their functionality. The calling into question of symbolic language is a key strategy of rhetorical discourse. In essence, scholars must be aware of language and its power to define, not only in the discourses of reading and writing; scholars must see the rhetorical and ideological significance of film. Moreover, as scholars continue to examine black films, with effective and appropriate epistemological frameworks, a greater appreciation of black film will emerge. If these arguments are evidence for the rhetorical and cultural importance of the films, then it is incumbent that the researcher examines both Lee's *Bamboozled* (2000) and *X* (1992).

Aims of the Study

The aim of any study is to push ideas to their breaking point or to challenge past scholarship with a critical inquiry. This dissertation is no different; its aims and objectives are just as noble. The researcher examines black identity from a rhetorical paradigm. Instead of limiting black identity to a core set of logocentric assumptions and rhetorical theories, this study acknowledges that identity is part of a confluence of social forces, which is always acculturating. Last, the researcher also poses a perspective in which to examine black identity and negotiation. Thus, the aim of this dissertation is to demystify concepts and manifestations of essentialism and interrogate notions of assimilation.

Outline of the Chapters

Chapter I is the introductory chapter. It sets the tone and framework for the entire document. It includes a discussion on the impetus for the study; it also includes the statement of the problem, significance of the study, research question, and role of the critic.

Chapter II discusses the critical method and theory. In addition to the critical method and theory, the chapter offers key terms critical to the study.

Chapter III focuses on the review of literature as it pertains and is significant to this study; it also includes a review of the method, film theory, and critical information regarding *Bamboozled* (2000) and *X* (1992).

Chapter IV represents the actual analysis of the films. Specific sections of the films are analyzed and categorized, providing a cultural and rhetorical foundation to address the research questions.

Chapter V addresses the research questions: How do Ready-to-sign cultural contracts, Quasi-completed cultural contracts, and Cocreated cultural contracts have an impact on black identity in the films

Bamboozled (2000) and *X* (1992)? What are the consequences for breaching contracts in the films *Bamboozled* (2000) and *X* (1992)?

Chapter VI summarizes findings and makes suggestions for future studies.

II
Theoretical Framework and Methodology

As mentioned in Chapter I, the study of black identity is intricate and, for the purposes of this research, it calls upon the employment of a cluster of critical theories to tease out the nuances that make the issue of black identity a highly complex phenomenon. In short, the theories utilized are key in the various parts of the analysis and are co-dependent with one another, as they work together to bring into fruition a careful and critical analysis of black identity and negotiation in Spike Lee's *Bamboozled* (2000) and *X* (1992).

Complicity of Negative Difference

Rhetorically, the implications of McPhail's (1996a) theory allow for a person to understand the communicative dimensions of a social interaction, how people's presuppositions are plagued with essentialism and undergird their evaluations and interactions with others. McPhail's (1996a) theory speaks to these underlying obstacles that serve as epistemological frameworks to understand identity. These obstacles are found in the complex network of negative difference. The researcher will elaborate briefly on negative difference and its significance to McPhail's (1996a) theory and the research.

Negative difference is a specific tool that amplifies the importance of a human's ability to create xenophobic attitudes toward culture and difference. Negative difference also allows for the belief that one system of logic is better than another. As such, a person can carry the attitude that one way of knowing is far better than another (McPhail, 1996a). Negative difference, in this light, allows humans to create essentialist truths and act accordingly to these truths. To this end, negative difference can construct crude linguistic relationships about any entity, which may be fabricated, and make it real. Because negative difference examines the essence of phenomena, the essence of phenomena can be understood in terms of the strategic utilization of language.

Language, in this line of thinking, is a critical component to McPhail's (1996a) theory because it deals with issues of representation and truth as discussed in the films *Bamboozled* (2000) and *X* (1992). McPhail's (1991) theory of complicity to negative difference suggests that in any discourse, idea, or theory, there is complicity to a perceived logic, which is the equivalent to an essentialist truth and grounded in misrepresentation. In turn, these essentialist truths of representation often guide individuals' communicative interaction with one another. Because essentialist truths often go unnoticed, McPhail's (1996a) theory of complicity challenges and unearths the various formations of essentialist discourse. According to McPhail (1996a), "The calling into question of this language of negative difference has become a key strategy in many feminist, afrocentric, and rhetorical theories of discourse" (p. 2). By focusing on the essentialist and complicit nature of language, issues of gender, race, and ideology are located.

Essentialist thinking is not merely the ideological representations of gender, race, and so forth. Essentialism includes complicity to any logocentric thinking, without regard for other epistemological frameworks; it is the failure to be self-reflexive or aware of a person's decisions and bias. In other words, essentialism reflects a person's values and beliefs. McPhail (1991) noted, "The analysis of complicity as a theory of negative difference is rooted in the linguistic theories articulated by the ancient Greek Sophists...whose theory of opposite party clearly illustrates the problem of complicity as it functions in...discourse" (p. 2).

Consider, for example, the Sophists and some of the Greek philosophers. Complicity in discourse can be found in both the Greek philosophers and the Sophist logocentric preference for philosophy and rhetoric. McPhail (1996a) noted that Plato and many of the Greek philosophers carried a disdain for rhetoric because it wasn't guided by wisdom; therefore, rhetoric couldn't lead to truth, just opinion. The Sophists favored rhetoric because of its pragmatic and practical value toward knowledge. As such, rhetoric provided a type of relative knowledge that lead to a fruitful participation in public life. McPhail (1991) noted:

> Logocentrism is profoundly interrelated in Western discourse as old as the Phaedrus of Plato, in which one finds the earliest figures of blackness as an absence, a figure of negation. Blackness as a figure of negation points to an essential difference intimately connected to the assumptions of knowledge in Western discourse. (p. 3)

Essentialism does not solely rest in the Sophistic and Platonic dialogues; it can be found in the choices that individuals make. Individuals can be led to believe that Afrocentric methods are useless because they are seldom chosen or that they remain invisible in communication departments and communication textbooks (Jackson, 2002). Essentialism in this context is a result of individuals' acculturated and encultured social practices, which become naturalized. As such, essentialism is the positioning of one logic over another.

McPhail (1991) also noted that essentialism is a result of presumptions and half-truths, which are based on probability are crystallized as truths in individuals' daily lives. These truths, which are normalized, dominate people's thought process and exist as unchallenged thoughts and practices. McPhail (1991) asserted:

> Essentialism, which is the dominant epistemological position articulated in Western culture, posits a reality in which material and symbolic processes exist in and of themselves. This results in linguistics practices which legitimate argumentative and critical discourse, precisely because such discourse is aimed at the discovery of essential truths. (p. 2)

In review, McPhail's (1991) theory represents the following:
- It encourages a critical investigation into the complicity of Western essentialist discourse, a discourse that utilizes a variety of rhetorical strategies to buttress its claim to truth.
- Moreover, McPhail's method is increasingly distrustful of language to convey a single authoritarian message.
- Last, the problem with language for McPhail is that it attempts to exclude. In doing so, language ignores, represses, and marginalizes some concepts while upholding others. To this end, McPhail sees language as the study of limitations.

Cultural Contract Theory of Negotiation

Jackson's (2002) theory consists of three components, which are understood as cultural contracts: Ready-to-sign, Quasi-completed, and Cocreated. These three function as a set of ideological restraints that a person is forced to assimilate. Jackson (2002) maintained, "The term 'cultural contracts' refers to the end product of identity negotiation; hence every 'signed' or agreed-upon cultural contract has a direct impact on one's identity" (p. 49).

Negotiation is key in Jackson's (2002) quote. "Negotiation" is a term implying process of deliberation; therefore, scholars can come to an understanding that identity is a process of formation and transformation. Another dimension of Jackson's (2002) theory is a "breached contract." A breached or broken contract refers to the transition from one contract to another contract. Broken contracts occur because one party refuses to assimilate to the preexisting stipulations of the contract: "As with any negotiation, one can either abide by an existing contractual arrangement, change the terms of the contract if permissible, or choose another contract" (Jackson, 2002, p. 50). The fundamental purpose of Jackson's (1999) theory is to gain further insight into the process of cultural identity negotiation. To negotiate identity implies that identity formation be considered a communication phenomenon among two or more individuals that are driven by message exchange over a period of time.

Hecht, Collier, and Ribeau (1993) suggested, "Identity is created by the individual and is cocreated [over time] as people come into contact with one another and the environment. As people align themselves with various groups, this co-creation process is negotiated" (p. 30). Over time, a personal identity and social identity evolve. Both the personal identity and the social identity will be explored clearly.

James Baldwin (1974), in his seminal work *If Beale Street Could Talk,* described the inner conflict of personal identity and social identity. As the issue of race confronts Tish, a character in Baldwin's (1974) novel, Tish is aware of the difference between herself and others. This awareness of race makes her a stranger to herself. Although Tish is fictitious, her accounts speak volumes about the negotiation process of her personal identity, which she is aware of due to race. Baldwin (1974) doesn't offer any solution to this issue. The best Tish can do is learn how to negotiate and maintain her personal identity.

The same stands true for the negotiation process of individuals' own identity in any communicative situation. This doesn't assume that individuals must strive for a balance or that a balance is possible. Much of people's identity is still changing. Each part of a person's identity is in competition with the other. Part of negotiating an individual's identity is not predicting when, where, and which identity will take precedence over the other. By understanding the complexity of identity, people begin to understand why one type of identity dominates the other. In other words, people are bound to negotiate their identity, and people have the agency in the negotiation process—that is, they have the ability to decide how much of their identity they want to negotiate and when negotiation may or may not be beneficial. As mentioned before, cultural contracts can always be breached. In other words, cultural contracts do not negate agency. Quite the opposite, it is always a person's choice to exit a contract for another.

Social identity directly relates to the contract that a person has signed; it is largely based on context, as all contracts are. The context may be a university, church, or any given organization. Social identity is the group identity, which both parties deem valuable (Jackson, 2002). It is based on pure assimilation. Assimilation is the concerted effort to erase the politics of difference between cultures. A social identity alludes to a homogeneous relationship among various interactants. The irony is that although the interactants are heterogeneous, as they begin to assimilate, they become homogeneous.

Forging this relationship are language and culture. Jackson (2002) submitted, "Identity is defined by the individual and is cocreated as people come into contact with one another and the environment" (p. 50). Ostensibly, there is semblance between people's culture and the language they use. Language becomes an index of people's social construct, impaling their ideology, decision making, and actions (Wright & Hailu, 1989). As such, identity is the end product of the negotiation process.

In summary, Jackson's (2002) theory is particularly interesting because it does the following:

- Jackson's theory examines the intracultural dynamics among participants.
- Moreover, Jackson's theory does not make a distinction between who is doing the signing and who is composing the contract. Any one person can be responsible for the creation and signing of the contract.
- The value in the aforementioned method is that it is malleable and fluid. There is a reciprocal relationship between identity and the contract. As identity changes, so does the contract. Scholars know this because Hall and Gay (1996) reported that identity is blurred, nonlinear, and a complex fusion of public demands and personal wills. Even after the acculturation process, identity negotiation is an ongoing dynamic because culture changes, human interactions change, and most important, language is always evolving.
- Last, to accept this idea, people must accept that personal identity and social identity are communicative phenomena and must be understood as a series of morphologies. In short, Jackson's theory contributes to a critical exploration of identity, but specifically black identity and its negotiation.

As mentioned previously, different theories will be used for different functions. Jackson (2002) and McPhail (1996a), for example, serve as the theories that the researcher will use to analyze the films and essentialist discourse, and place the discourse into cultural contracts. The theories in the next section are critical theories used to address the research questions. The theories are West's (1993) "alienation," Du Bois' (1903) "double-consciousness," and Watts' (2002) "hermeneutical ethos."

Alienation

For Cornel West (1993), there are two key points to his notion of "alienation": "alienation" as a black existential struggle and "alienation" as an ideological system of oppression.

The first principle of West's (1993) theory suggests that African Americans must face the possibility of strained realities. Within the same principle of reasoning, each African American must somehow resolve this conflict individually for him- or herself. The impetus of this turmoil is to be found first in white dominant culture, which cannot be ignored, and second, in the ethnic black culture of his or her group. This leads to more than a quandary as alluded to in Du Bois' (1903) theory. "Alienation," according to West (1993), is an existential journey of conflict. It emphasizes the following common themes: question of identity, the experience of choice, and the absence of rational understanding of the universe with a consequent dread or sense of absurdity in human life (West, 1993). The combination of these themes suggests an emotional tone or mood. The history of the African American is a semblance of these themes mentioned by West. West characterized the African American as lost between two worlds of existence. West's (1993) theory suggests that the present day African American's task is to find his or her own existence. Once he or she finds it, he or she will have a voice. Because of the existential turmoil, West's theory positions African-American identity as a discontinuous process of social demands. If scholars are to examine "alienation" as discontinuous points of identity, then African-American identity is subject to the continuous play of history, culture, and power. West (1993) submitted that black identities are identities that are unstable points of identification. As such, African-American identity is fluctuating and synthetic.

West's (1993) theory of "alienation" brings into view the communicative dilemma of how social exigencies affect black identity; it also has relevance to the issues of breached contracts. Beyond the epistemological tenets of West's (1993) theory, his theory provides a specific ontological claim that has a direct impact for this particular study. If black identity is understood as pastiche, then the nature of black identity can be expressed as a feeling of uncertainty and possibly "alienation." West (1993) noted:

> The modern black diasporan problematic of invisibility and namelessness can be understood as the condition of relative lack of black power to represent themselves to themselves and others as complex human beings, and thereby to context the bombardment of negative, degrading stereotypes put forward by white supremacist ideologies. (p. 16)

In short, West's (1993) theory of "alienation" describes the struggle of the African American as one that is existential.

The second principle of "alienation" is "alienation" as a category of oppressive systems. In this mode of thinking, "alienation" is a set of oppressive structures that aim to distance an individual from his or her culture. According to West (1993), this is done through the control of language and ideology. As such, "alienation" is articulated as any wide ranging systems of beliefs, ways of thoughts, and categories that provide the foundation of control (West, 1993). For example, West (1993) examined the condition of the slaves who were brought to America. These slaves were stripped of their language, religion, and family. These conditions were intentionally set up to oppress the slaves and distance them from what is familiar. West (1993) noted that the African American is alienated insofar as he or she cannot understand or accept him- or herself (West, 1993). The African American is alienated from his or her desire insofar as he or she is not authentically his or her own. In other words, the African American is alienated because he or she does not feel in control of his or her own culture (West, 1993).

In review, the central point of West's (1993) theory is "alienation," both existential and ideological. West (1993) discusses "alienation" within two contexts: "alienation" as an existential struggle, and "alienation" as an ideological system of oppression:

- The first principle of alienation is "alienation" as an existential struggle because African Americans face the possibility of strained realities. Each African American must solve this conflict for him- or herself.
- The second principle of "alienation" is "alienation" as a category of oppressive systems. In this mode of thinking, alienation is a set of oppressive structures that aim to distance an individual from his or her culture. According to West (1993), this is done through the control of language and ideology.

Double-Consciousness

In 1903, Du Bois published the book *The Souls of Black Folk*. In this book, he described his theory of "double-consciousness." "Double-consciousness" describes the racial dilemma that confronts all blacks—the racial divide. Dubois' theory describes two types of striving for African Americans. These strivings are the desire to be accepted by mainstream culture by means of assimilation and Black Nationalism. The researcher will describe the first account, followed by the second account.

> It is a peculiar sensation, this double-consciousness, this sense of always looking at one's self through the eyes of others, of measuring one's soul by the tape of a world.... One ever feels his twoness–an American, a Negro; two souls, two thoughts, two unreconciled strivings; two warring ideals in one dark body, whose dogged strength alone keeps it from being torn asunder. (Du Bois, 1903, p. 3)

This passage is the foundation of Du Bois' (1903) theory as it highlights the notion of difference. For Du Bois (1903), black identity is a concept based on perceived inequity. The perceived inequity creates a social and psychological distance from one's self and others. The black who experiences a "double-consciousness" lives in a state of strife for which he or she blames culture (Du Bois, 1903). He or she is trapped in a maze of his or her own consciousness and at times is overly conscious. In many ways, the weight of his or her thoughts leaves him or her paralyzed. According to Du Bois (1903), these frustrating feelings center on the need for blacks to belong and to feel secure. Du Bois (1903) noted,

> Between me and the other world there is an unasked question: unasked by some through feelings of delicacy; by others through the difficulty of rightly framing it. All nevertheless, flutter round it. They approach me in a half-hesitant sort of way, eye me curiously or compassionately, and then, instead of saying directly, How does it feel to be a problem? (p. 44)

This quote clearly identifies the intercultural problem that blacks face with whites. Thinking of one's self as a problem or different is the beginning of a "double-consciousness" because a person is always examining him- or herself through his or her own eyes and through the eyes of others. More important, because each culture is different, differences will always exist. These differences are not deficiencies, but if a person is to measure him- or herself by the values of another culture, then he or she is bound to feel contempt and inadequate. Du Bois (1903) stated,

> Then it dawned upon me with a certain suddenness that I was different from the others; or like, mayhap, in heart and life and longing, but shut out from their world by a vast veil. I had thereafter no desire to tear down that veil, to creep through; I held all beyond it in common contempt...in a region of blue sky and great wandering shadows. (p. 44)

Du Bois (1903) described this longing to belong through the metaphoric veil. Du Bois (1903) saw the veil as an amalgam of distinctions (e.g., between race, politics, and education), which marginalizes one group and uplifts the other. Du Bois (1903) noted that the African American has created a relentless aim to "satisfy two unreconciled ideals, has wrought havoc, and has ultimately sent [African-Americans] often wooing false gods and invoking false means of salvation, and at times even seemed about to make them ashamed of themselves" (p. 13).

In short, Du Bois' (1903) theory of "double-consciousness" examines a cultural and political quagmire unique to blacks. Second, the theory describes African-American identity through Du Bois' (1903) example of the veil. The veil is critical to Du Bois' (1903) theory because it articulates the intercultural dilemma facing both whites and blacks.

The researcher will examine the second facet of Du Bois' (1903) theory: Black Nationalism. Du Bois (1903) saw blacks as a culture that is torn asunder by its own members. According to Du Bois (1903), there is a feeling of self-hate that pervades black culture. This feeling is not innate; it was cultivated through racist discourse implemented by hegemonic structures. The perpetuation of self-hate creates division among its people and prevents blacks from achieving solidarity. Education is needed to remedy the problem. Du Bois (1903) noted that education is key to Black Nationalism. "Black Nationalism" is a term that describes an "all-black party" that has financial, political, and social influence in the affairs of mainstream culture. Within the framework of Du Bois (1903) theory, Black Nationalism is the key to prosperity. Black Nationalism is a form of self-determination. It is the belief that a person or people can provide adequately for themselves.

In review, there are two major components to Du Bois' (1903) theory: assimilation and Black Nationalism.

- First, assimilation assumes that blacks want equal and nondiscriminatory treatment from whites. In other words, they want to be treated in the same manner as whites. Longing to fit in, they are often excluded because of their skin color. And in trying to assimilate to mainstream culture, they are often met with rancor from their own culture. The rejection from both white and black culture leaves the black in a quandary. This quandary is otherwise known as a "double-consciousness."
- Second, Black Nationalism ideally states that unification among blacks is possible. Although blacks are torn asunder by having two souls and two irreconcilable aims, Black Nationalism is a philosophy of unification. This philosophy encourages self-reliance and responsibility for one's self and for the collective culture.

Hermeneutical Ethos

Watts' (2002) theory of "hermeneutical ethos" has specific implications for the progressive African American forecast in Locke's (1925) text, *The New Negro*. Briefly, Locke provided a romantic picture of the progressive African American. The progressive African American is a person who is fully aware of him- or herself and who is fully adaptable in all communicative situations. The researcher will discuss the central idea important to a "hermeneutical ethos."

The pivotal point critical to Watts' (2002) theory is that it seeks to produce practical, pragmatic knowledge that is judged by the degree of historical situatedness and its ability to produce praxis, or action. Within this line of reasoning, a "hermeneutical ethos" is an interpretive process; it seeks to understand how a person can best handle him- or herself as a competent human being, in social interactions, and in decision making.

Enveloped in Watts' (2002) theory is a sense of romanticism juxtaposed with a sense of realism. Romanticism for Watts (2002) was the impetus for a "hermeneutical ethos." Romanticism provides the vision and motivation for action. Realism, on the other hand, provides a premise or grounding for the carrying out of the act. Watts (2002) suggested that these two components provide a basic structure for human understanding: "This structure is temporal and is less a formation than a forming, changing, or becoming. Hermeneutical knowledge is predicated on our capacity to make sense of our shifting lived experiences, a capacity that, though ontological, is mediated by language" (p. 20).

A "hermeneutical ethos" implies a new way of understanding, as a person makes use of the interpretive process. According to Watts (2002), a "hermeneutical ethos" has to do more with pragmatics and one's ability to make the best possible decision to conduct one's life. Moreover, hermeneutics, a system of pragmatic query, makes clear and appraises the value of the idea, its merits and flaws, and makes the best possible judgment about a communicative intention or act (Watts, 2002).

Locke's (1925) vision is the end result of Watts' (2002) epistemology: a hermeneutical [ethos] is an interpretive activity that begins and ends with the essential questioning of people's everyday being with others. This questioning is about how best to conduct one's personal affairs within a field of conflicting and fluid relations and is instigated by one's social world and shaped by it.

In short, a "hermeneutical ethos" addresses how a person can resolve conflicting and paradoxical points of view that affect his or her identity and the way he or she chooses to deal with conflicting communication styles, behaviors, and cultural beliefs. In many ways, a "hermeneutical ethos" is a framework in which people can achieve balance and harmony with others and themselves. Most important, a "hermeneutical ethos" situates itself in the field of praxis. Watts (2002) saw "hermeneutical ethos" meaningful in that it can be applied to real life situations. Watts (2002) maintained, a "hermeneutical ethos" is guided "by one's sense of the proper orchestration, and articulation of topical material in accordance with one's lived experience" (p. 22). The implication here is that after a person achieves a level of understanding

or communicative competence, he or she is able to exercise a level of wisdom in decision making and application. Concisely, Watts' (2002) theory communicates the following points:
- The pivotal point critical to Watts' (2002) theory is that it seeks to produce practical, pragmatic knowledge that is judged by the degree of historical situatedness.
- A "hermeneutical ethos" opens the lines of communication. In effect, a "hermeneutical ethos" allows both parties to transcend their individual thinking patterns and achieve mutual consent.
- A "hermeneutical ethos" is meaningful in that it can be applied to real life situations.

Justification for Multiple Theories

The basic principle that all of the theories hold is that language is more than a tool that people use to communicate; once the interpretive process begins, language becomes a significant part of people's everyday experience in which individuals come to understand themselves. It is on this basis that humans make decisions and act accordingly. As such, through language individuals begin to define themselves in relation to others (Roy & Starosta, 2001). Moreover, language is the vehicle through which individuals relate to the past, understand the present, and ruminate about the future.

Briefly, all of the theories utilized in this study examine language as a focal point to understanding identity; they contend that identity and representation are not a transient issue, here today and gone tomorrow, but are forms of power and control. Roy and Starosta (2001) maintained, "Power is an important feature in all social/(gradations) interactions because it both sets the limits of and affords the possibilities for human action" (p. 13). Roy and Starosta's (2001) statement touches upon the multilayered and fluid nature of language and power. Like relationships and identity, ideology is present in various levels. Therefore, the goal is to make sense of the dynamic relationship, coexisting between language, power, and identity. If ideology and identity are to be understood by this analogy, then the theories are likened to a drill, penetrating through the various layers of black identity. Jackson's (2002), McPhail's (1996a), West's (1993), Du Bois' (1903), and Watts' (2002) theories serve as the drills that penetrate through the communicative problems of black identity.

As a group, the theories aid the researcher in a detailed understanding of the research problem. The collaboration of the theories makes way for a fruitful discussion and analysis. Martin and Nakayama (1999) communicated that the process of using multiple theories enhances the researcher's understanding of the issue. Interparadigmatic borrowing, the collaborative effort of joining seemingly disparate theories, is quite normal in the communication field. Communication theory in its most infant and mature stage is heterogeneous; it is a fruition of cultural studies, psychology, critical studies, philosophy, and other disciplines. Littlejohn (1996) reported that communication is central and rooted in various disciplines in socio-scientific discourse.

Interparadigmatic borrowing is an effective means of understanding communicative issues that retains its authenticity as a communicative issue. Martin and Nakayama (1999) provided an analogy: "This traveling is analogous to a traveler abroad learning new cultural ways that they incorporate into their lives back home. However, the researcher, while borrowing, is still fundamentally committed to research with a particular paradigm" (p. 12). Interparadigmatic borrowing is an approach that is quite competent to provide depth and latitude to the research problems; it sees the nature of the issue as a complex semblance of communicative forces and addresses the issue in a critical manner.

Methodology

Methods are strategic procedures that the researcher uses to explore and investigate the problems. They are logical steps that the researcher follows and, in doing so, the researcher is able to make judgments about the phenomenon. Methods are influenced by the theories that drive them. For example, when using a critical theory, the method should comply with the theory. To this end, the methodology used in this study is critical as it reflects the type of theories utilized:

1. Using McPhail's (1991) theory of negative difference, the researcher will locate essentialist and rhetorical messages. These essentialist messages are found in select dialogues and scenes.
2. Messages stereotyping the characters in the films *Bamboozled* (2000) and *X* (1992) are dislocated from the text and analyzed.
3. Once the films are analyzed for their essentialist significance, the discourse is then placed into Jackson's cultural contracts.
4. The researcher decides which contract will adjoin the character by the distribution of power exhibited in the communicative interaction between characters. By the distribution of power, the researcher means *who* is controlling the language of the other. In doing so, the ideological grammar of the characters comes into being.
5. Upon analyzing the characters within the framework of cultural contracts, various ways blacks negotiate their identity comes into fruition. The information from cultural contracts allows the researcher to address the research questions.

III
Literature Review

The literature presented is appropriate and specific for the rhetorical issue and the problem at hand. The literature is divided into sections. The sections are Literature Review of Black Cinema, Rhetorical Texts Pertaining to the Content of Films, and Literature Review of Identity. Each section provides the reader with a framework to aid in the comprehension and understanding of the critical subject matter.

Literature Review of Black Cinema

Black American Cinema by Manthia Diawara (1993) examines black American cinema from two perspectives: an aesthetic perspective (e.g., inclusive of utopian idealism and Black Nationalism) and from a critical perspective (e.g., how blacks are portrayed, how blacks' images contribute to a larger understanding of who they are). As such, the text captures the psychology and motive behind the development of black cinema. Last, the text comments briefly on a critical and imperative perspective of black cinema—the auteur.

Of significance to the research project is the section on aesthetics and new realism. This section is extremely vital because it addresses how white realism is used as a discourse to present portrayals of blacks. A film such as D.W. Griffith's *The Birth of a Nation* (1915) is an excellent example of realism and essentialism.

Slow Fade to Black by Thomas Cripps (1977) examines the history of race, mediated via cinema. The text examines properties of assimilation, claiming that assimilation paved the way for African-American cinema. Cripps' (1977) text explores what it means for African-American films to assimilate into mainstream culture. To assimilate means to fit into the pejorative landscapes envisioned by white producers. Second, Cripps' (1977) text is significant because it identifies the dilemma for black actors. This dilemma is closely related to what W.E.B. Du Bois (1903) termed "double-consciousness." African-American actors face the possibility of having two identities, both of which are in discord with one another. Cripps (1977) noted that in 1942, there was a written agreement reached by the delegates of the National Association for the Advancement of Colored People and the heads of Hollywood studios. This event made a concerted effort to take African-American actors out of their identity negotiation dilemma. Cripps (1977) noted, "The studio agreed to abandon pejorative racial roles, to place Negroes in positions as extras they could reasonably be expected to occupy in society, and to begin the slow task of integrating Blacks into the ranks of studio technicians" (p. 56). Meaningful for the qualities noted previously, Cripps' (1977) text provides a historical account of essentialist and racist discourse, promulgated by Hollywood.

Blaxploitation Films by Mikel J. Koven (2001) discusses the central tenants indicative of blaxploitation films. The text provides examples of several films that demonstrate exploitive qualities. Koven (2001) submitted that "Blaxploitation films exploit our desire to see black people, specifically, African Americans, on screen, doing presumably what one expects or wants to see African Americans doing" (p. 7). The text examines the psyche behind the making of these films, which is to say the dreams and aspirations sold and distributed to an audience willing to pay for them. Blaxploitation films of the late sixties and seventies depicted a reality about the world that African Americans could identify with, even if the stories themselves were purely fantasy. Koven's book serves as an introduction to this genre of cinema.

Redefining Black Films by Mark Reid (1993) poses several questions about black films and their origins. Reid (1993) differentiated between black commercial film and black independent film. Clearly, the distinction between the two is worth mentioning. Works understood as black film categorize and limit the genre to films containing black people. Other works also identified as black film assume that because the director is black, the film is black. In reality, a black film is postured in the history of black discourse and worldview. It acknowledges differences within the black diaspora. For the life of black cinema, white and black directors alike fail to recognize important characteristics of black identity. By failure to understand polemical differences, producers perpetuate stereotypes, adding to gross misconceptions about black culture. Reid's book adds value to the researcher's appraisal of black film theory, elements of black cinema, and its function and purpose.

Rhetorical Texts Pertaining to the Content of Films
X

X (1992) is a docudrama that centers on the historical figure Malcolm X. Of central interest to this research is not only Lee's reconstruction and narrative account of Malcolm X (Malcolm X's involvement with the Nation of Islam, his personal relationship with Elijah Muhammad, his pilgrimage to Mecca, and his return from Mecca) but the cultural contracts emanating throughout these stages of his life.

Cultural contracts communicate the negotiation and transformation of identity. Evidence of contract and identity negotiation is apparent in Lee's interpretation of the rhetoric of Malcolm X and his change in communicative strategies. These all are indicative of a transformed worldview. This newfound worldview isolated Malcolm, catapulting him into another cultural/rhetorical dimension. Malcolm's new cultural rhetorical contract can be understood as "alienation." "Alienation" describes communicative and existential transformation. Moreover, "alienation" has specific implications for the transition period from one contract to another, with particular attention to identity.

Understanding Malcolm X: The Controversial Changes in His Political Philosophy by Edward Leader (1993) critically evaluates the philosophy of Malcolm's rhetoric from 1960–1965. It does not painstakingly deliberate over Malcolm's disposition toward whites. The text categorically investigates his political philosophy. Leader (1993) maintained, "Political philosophy tells us how to find out where we stand and where we may be going; it gives some answers to these questions; it prepares us for the possibilities of the future" (p. 19). Implicit in Leader's (1993) comment are the dynamics of cultural contracts; Leader speaks to the various gradations of systemic and ideological adaptation. Malcolm unequivocally exhausted several contracts as he meandered through several ideological schools of thought. Leader's (1993) text provides an informative take on the various ideological shifts that Malcolm embraced.

"Colonizing the Borderlines: Shifting Circumference in the Rhetoric of Malcolm X" by Robert E. Terrill (2000) highlights the last year of Malcolm's life, with attention on Malcolm's change in ideology. During Malcolm's last years, he was forced to compose a rhetorical framework that consisted of racial and economic inclusion. Terrill (2000) submitted, "Framing such a view, and then inviting an audience to share it, illustrates not an actual accomplishment but also the emancipatory potential of rhetoric" (p. 68). In addition to adapting a new rhetoric, Malcolm asked his audience to adopt a new worldview and to revamp their identities. Of key importance to the researcher is the rhetorical and negotiatory process described by Terrill (2000).

Malcolm X Speaks: Selected Speeches and Statements by George Breitman (1982) examines several of Malcolm's most influential speeches. More specifically, the text examines Malcolm as a political figure, whose involvement with the black liberationist movement inspired an anti-imperialist movement. For Malcolm, the anti-imperial movement was a nonviolent approach toward the rehabilitation of the negro in America. It is based on the deconstruction of the Eurocentric paradigm—its language, discourse, and worldview. Because African Americans had been denied their religion, language, culture, and heritage, the black liberationist movement reestablished a connection between the negro and his or her culture. The text is beneficial because it articulates cogent arguments for African Americans to reconnect with their history and culture.

"The Brand X of Post Negritude Frontier" by Mark A. Reid (1995) uses postnegritude theory to evaluate Malcolm's nonviolent discourse. "Postnegritude" is an ideology of empowerment. Its goal is to restore cultural dignity and pride to its people. A sub-point of "postnegritude" theory is Black Nationalism, which was a critical component to Malcolm's discourse. Black Nationalism is a political ideology and movement among African Americans that stresses African-derived economic values, independence, and racial unity. For Malcolm, Black Nationalism was based on the premise that blacks are systematically oppressed by white society. Reid's (1995) article shed light on the rhetorical and ideological prowess of Malcolm's discourse.

"Malcolm X Across the Genres (motion picture 'X' and book 'The Autobiography of Malcolm X')" by Irvin Painter (1993) discusses Lee's feature film *X* (1992). According to Painter (1993), the film closely followed the Nation of Islam and their effect on the psyche of the African American. The author examined Lee's (1992) depiction of Malcolm's rhetoric. Malcolm's racialized ideology sought to end White European influence in black Africa—both political and by colonial governments. The separatist doctrine of ethnic pride was not anti-Semitic. Rather, Malcolm's rhetoric was a source of agency and self-reliance. More important, the article examined Malcolm's rhetoric as nonassimilationist in that it would dilute Malcolm's ethic as a leader. As such, the article is beneficial in that it analyzes the rhetoric of Malcolm, seen through the eyes of Lee.

Bamboozled

Bamboozled (2000) starts where *X* ends. The term *bamboozled* was used by Malcolm to illustrate white corporate American management, manipulation of ideology, and discourse within the public sphere. In the opening scene of *Bamboozled*, Malcolm's voice is clearly heard: "You have been hoodwinked…bamboozled." This film centers on the "bamboozled effect" of blacks and how that, in turn, shapes and defines black identity. Lee most brilliantly articulated this through the use of three characters: Delacroix, Cheeba, and Mantan.

Of central interest to this film are the ideological representations of the "bamboozled effect" and the silent ideologies, voicing essentialist facets of perceived black identity. As in the film *X*, Lee used traditional black themes (e.g., relationships, gender issues) as a starting point to bring into fruition essentialist characteristics of black identity. Lee did this through what McPhail (1991) termed "negative difference." McPhail (1991) defined "negative difference" as "the principle of critical analysis that undergirds essentialist epistemology" (p. 2). As he did in *X*, Lee positioned characters into cultural contracts that challenged and called into question issues of identity.

"Race, Media and Money: A Critical Symposium on Spike Lee's 'Bamboozled'" by Cynthia Lucia (2001) examines minstrel shows, Lee's effective use of the shows to articulate complicity from both the audience in the film and the viewers of the film. Lucia (2001) complied with Lee that as the audience laughed at the blackface, blacks laughed along; therefore, blacks are complicit. The exploration of complicity, as it relates to racist stereotypes, is critical to the investigation of the issues. Moreover, Lucia's (2001) analysis harmonizes with McPhail's (1996a) complicity of negative difference theory. Lucia (2001) underscored the double-bonded contract implicit within complicity and drew attention to blaxploitation as a social recourse.

"Nowhere Left to Stand: The Burnt Cork Root of Popular Culture" by Michael Rogin (2001) examines white culture's fascination with black identity after the Civil War. As an attempt to gain access to black culture, whites deemed it appropriate to understand black culture through imagery, with varying satirical images communicating hate, disdain, and ridicule. Rogin's (2001) article also examines American culture and its need to produce racy television shows. With emphasis on the need to gain audience viewership, Rogin (2001) exposed the ethical dimension of television broadcasting and broadcasters' decision to compromise what may or may not be ethical for higher ratings. Rogin (2001) provided the researcher with an understanding of complicity, how it is disguised and marketed through entertainment.

"Thinking About the Power of Images: An Interview with Spike Lee" by Gary Crowdus and Dan Georakas (2001) examines the relationship between race and ideology in *Bamboozled*. In particular, Lee reconceptualized blackface to mean a compromising of the self, not just putting on burnt cork. Lee (2000) said, "Of course no one uses blackface any more. It's gotten more sophisticated. Gangsta rap videos, a lot of TV shows on UPN and WB—a lot of us are still acting as buffoons and coons" (p. 10). The article by Crowdus and Georakas (2001) grapples with the political aspect of identity. Through the use of cultural artifacts (black and white collectible dolls), Lee chronicled the history of black identity in film. Lee (2000) stated that it is a reminder of "how we were viewed in the past and possibly still are today" (p. 9).

"Bamboozled: White Supremacy and a Black Way of Being Human" by Greg Tate (2001) examines the representation of African Americans in the entertainment industry. Tate (2001) explored blackness and slavery through symbolic representations of compromise. The question of what is ethically sacrificed in trading blackness for personal gain is the question of significance for Tate. Implicit in Lee's question is assimilation and identity: How does one feel pride about being black and at the same time not feel alien in a culture that carries disdain for blacks? *Bamboozled* examines black life from a white perspective. Whites relate to black culture through freak shows, which give them reasons to feel better about themselves. The scenes in which Dunwitty attempts to define blackness by sports-trivia questions and clichés speak to the way that blacks are understood in *Bamboozled*.

"'Bamboozled' by Blackness: Movie Review *Bamboozled* by Spike Lee" by Cristy Tondeur (2001) explores the façade that diversity has been mistaken for multiculturalism. Blacks have been hoodwinked insofar as thinking that they are equals and first class citizens. Lee poignantly played on the word "bamboozled" as a direct indictment on blacks for buying into equality and multiculturalism. Diversity is mistaken for multiculturalism, which is the appreciation and positive reception of cultural differences. Diversity is the mere representation of multiculturalism, which consists of various cultural illustrations that all differ from one another. As such, Lee used a term by Malcolm X to show the relevance that "bamboozled" still has in contemporary culture.

"Identity, Power, and Local Television: African Americans, Organized Labor and UHF-TV in Chicago, 1962–1968" by Nathan Godfried (2002) examines the so-called "negro" as a subject of a freak show, inhumane and unnatural. Transformed by television, the negro continues to reinforce pejorative images of African Americans. According to Godfried (2002), when television producers were asked about the misrepresentation of African Americans, they reported, "We communicate what we see and what is apparently true." Godfried (2002) did not attempt to blame television producers; rather, with help from the Federal Communications Commission and other willing organizations, he sought to remedy the problem by educating, engaging in dialogue, and ultimately providing resources that contribute to education.

Literature Review of Identity

The *Ideologies of African American Literature: From the Harlem Renaissance to the Black Nationalist Revolt: A Sociology of Literature*

Perspective by E.R. Washington (2001) examines the ideological construction of black life in America; the book closely analyzes five different paradigms of thought, articulating pertinent information pertaining to African-American identity. For example, the text examines the narratives of Ralph Ellison and James Baldwin, who have written about black identity in America. In addition, Washington (2001) pointed out that Malcolm X's rhetoric of racial separatism and James Baldwin's rhetoric of racial inclusion sent mixed messages to the African-American community, which had a direct impact on the confusion of identity. An extremely significant function of this text is Washington's (2001) ability to provide the reader with a historical, political, and social climate in which to understand the rhetoric of identity and how it is negotiated.

Frantz Fanon's (1991) *Black Skin, White Masks* explores the social and historical foundations and psychological effect of colonialism and racism and discusses the pathologies arising from such acts. More specifically, the text explores the concept of "alienation" deriving from colonialism. For Fanon (1991), "alienation" bred self-hate among the imperialized, whose identity, values, and worldview become manipulated by their colonizer. Equally important, Fanon (1991) drew attention to the assimilation process, in which the colonized is forced to relinquish indigenous ideals and acquire new ones. Fanon's (1991) text is beneficial because it scrutinizes identity and the negotiatory process as a system of power, comprised of language and ideology. With emphasis on language, Fanon (1991) meticulously examined how language is both political and rhetorical.

Colonialism and Alienation: Concerning Frantz Fanon's Political Theory by Renate Zahar (1974) closely follows Fanon's (1991) theme of self-hate. According to Zahar (1974), self-hate is a psychological disposition that the colonizer inflicts on the colonized. As a result, the colonized mindset can only be understood as a series of psychological neuroses, contributing to unhealthy and negative feelings of self-hate; moreover, there is a paradox. As the colonized mimic the colonizer (psychological neurosis), the colonized begin to subjugate each other. What occurs beyond this paradox is the concept of "Negritude"; this is the crux of Fanon's (1991) thinking. "Negritude" is both a political movement and a philosophy, providing agency to the colonized. "Negritude" affirms autonomy and agency for the colonized. Because "Negritude" provides agency for blacks, blacks can see themselves not as the problem in society. Zahar (1974) stated, "The black man must be made to realize that his 'alienation' is not an individual problem. Its causes can be found in the interiorization of a historically and economically determined inferiority" (p. 28). Zahar (1974) continued, "If there is an inferiority complex, it is the outcome of a double process" (p. 28). The redeeming value in Fanon's (1991) text is two concepts: "Negritude" and "alienation." Both concepts speak to the complexity of identity, its negotiative process.

The Negotiation of Cultural Identity: Perceptions of European Americans and African Americans by Ronald Jackson (1999) examines various concepts of identity. Jackson (1999) examined identity through four research questions. These questions evaluate how both African Americans and European students see themselves and how they negotiate their own identity. Of key concern in Jackson's (1999) study are the historical understandings of identity, how the same problem still persists but the metaphors used to describe the problem change, and ultimately the current state of affairs for blacks. Jackson (1999) submitted that Du Bois (1903) described the negro with a "double-consciousness"; later, Fanon (1991) understood the problem as self-division. West (1993) quoted Du Bois as stating that blacks are in "a quest for white approval and acceptance, and an endeavor to overcome the internalized association of blackness with inferiority" (p. 18). Essentially, Jackson (1999) was communicating a rearticulation of the same issue. Resonating through these various narratives of identity and negotiation is the dialectic nature of language and power; there is seemingly a reciprocal between the two.

"Dessentializing Difference: Transformative Visions in Contemporary Black Thought" by Mark McPhail (2002) offers a transformative notion of identity. This goal is made possible by reexamining Du Bois' (1903) theory of "double-consciousness." McPhail (2002) noted that "the 'double-consciousness' might be read as a form of rhetorical coherence, a capacity to integrate diverse conception of reality that is grounded in the generative power of language" (p. 78). Rhetorical coherence reduces identity to an "amorphous formation"; it acknowledges the relationship between identity and language. Moreover, it deconstructs traditional concepts of whiteness and blackness as they relate to the politics of ethnicity. Clearly, McPhail's (2002) article holds that racism is a rhetorical problem. Racism is symbolically charged and fraught with ethnocentric notions. McPhail's (2002) article offers the researcher a transformative way of understanding identity, with emphasis on reconstruction; rhetorical coherence offers corrective measures for African Americans' identity, which is still torn.

"Intellectual Dislocation: Applying Analytic Afrocentricity to Narratives of Identity" by Molefi Asante (2002) examines the rhetorical chasm existing between Western discourse and Afrocentric discourse. Asante (2002) located the difference between the texts by their centeredness or decenteredness. Centeredness relates to the ideology that pervades the text. Decenteredness relates to application of decentering the discourse of oppression. Asante (2002) introduced "sentinel statements," which strategically clue in the Afrocentric scientist as to the types of centered discourse in the text. Asante (2002) then transcribed what can be understood as discourse analysis to a text to communicative interactions. By people understanding the centeredness (e.g., Eurocentric, Afrocentric, Asiocentric) in their own lives, they can make adjustments in their communication accordingly. Asante's (2002) article has direct impact on the researcher's ability to understand the dynamics and negotiation of one's identity.

The Rhetoric of Racism by Mark McPhail (1994) examines the relationship between language and the conceptualization of identity. It looks at rhetoric as the paintbrush used to draw the relationship. Within the realm of rhetoric, the very principle of essentialism makes way for racism to exist. McPhail (1994) noted, "A contemporary rhetorical theory of the language of racism suggests…the explanation for the fallacy of race" (p. 3). Signs coupled with symbols can distort, exaggerate, and misrepresent truth. They can take that which is visually fictional and make it real. McPhail (1994) noted, "Racism is an example of human symbolic and social interaction which has a number of rhetorical dimensions" (p. 4). McPhail's (1994) text aids the researcher in the connection between essentialism and identity existing in the films *X* (1992) and *Bamboozled* (2000).

"African American Ethos and Hermeneutical Rhetoric: An Exploration of Alain Locke's *The New Negro*" by Eric Watts (2002) examines Locke's (1925) conception of the "new negro." The "new negro" is a term Locke (1925) used to note certain global ethics that have transcendental value. Identity is no longer a concept that is dependent on social approbation and evaluation. The "new negro" defines himself according to an intrapersonal ethic. The text suggests that the "new negro" is metaphor for a "new soul"; it is the ability for the negro to transcend what Du Bois (1903) noted as "double-consciousness."

Watts (2002) argued that such a transformation is made possible by acquiring a "hermeneutical ethos." A "hermeneutical ethos" implies fusing theory with praxis: "Hermeneutic understanding is, thus, public and constitutive of emotional entailments of everyday lived experience" (Watts, 2002, p. 21). Watts' (2002) article not only aids the researcher in the development of the theoretical framework, but it also provides clarity to the African-American dilemma in the 21st century.

The Souls of Black Folk by W.E.B. Du Bois (1903) examines the 20th century issue of race: it speaks to the problem of race and identity affecting African Americans throughout the 20th century. Du Bois'

(1903) text is a displaced rhetorical argument, which is to say that it was too modern for its time. However, Dubois' text was insightful and prophetic because many of the ideas he talked about are current in the 21st century. The text is significant because it highlights the psychological tension that impales the existence of blacks. There exists a struggle: there is a search for interethnic validation within African-American culture, while blacks simultaneously try to locate themselves in the mainstream culture. The tension that exists is a rhetorical and intercultural problem. Du Bois' (1903) text critically examines that tension. It also aids the researcher in understanding identity and the negotiation process. Du Bois (1903) offered the metaphor, veil; this metaphor allows for a healthier interpretation of the issue.

Questions of Cultural Identity by Stuart Hall and Paul du Gay (1996) discusses the complex issue of identity. Both Hall and du Gay (1996) saw identity existing in multiple forms. For example, identity may be understood as a oneness. An individual may be aware of his or her existence, but being aware of his or her existence is dependent on that existence being confirmed by another individual. Hall and du Gay (1996) conceptualized identity as discontinuous points of identification. Identity can be discontinuous because it is always changing with new experiences. As such, identity is far from being fixed and ordered. Identity is the casual interplay and flux between social exigencies. The various types of identity function as coping mechanisms; they are ways in which individuals come to make sense out of the world in which they live. Hall and du Gay's (1996) text is a valuable resource, providing the researcher with various ways to conceptualize identity.

Keeping Faith: Philosophy and Race in America by Cornel West (1993) examines black identity as it relates to politics and education. West (1993) surveyed various issues that the black community deals with. Of specific concern to this research topic is West's (1993) use of the term "alienation." "Alienation," for West (1993), was a feeling of anxiety and abandonment that blacks face within mainstream culture. West (1993) described this feeling as the wandering or the aloofness of the soul that speaks to the modern "diasporan problem of invisibility and the namelessness, which can be understood as the condition of relative lack of black power to represent themselves and others as complex human beings...." (p. 16). What becomes seemingly clear is that "alienation" is part of a complex system of language. According to West (1993), once a culture's language is taken away, the culture's identity starts to dissipate. This text is vital to the researcher as it aids him in answering the research questions. West's (1993) articulation of "alienation" provides perspective and a context to understand the contemporary African-American struggle.

Literature Review

The literature cited is critical and necessary because of its impact toward this study. The literature review does three specific things: it provides a resource of information in areas of black cinema, an overview of the films analyzed, and vital information about black identity as it relates to this issue.

IV
Analysis

The following analysis is carried out in three parts. The first part consists of highlighting essentialist discourse in the films *Bamboozled* (2000) and *X* (1992). The rhetorical tool used in the analysis is McPhail's (1991) theory of complicity of negative difference. To reiterate a point of function, McPhail's (1991) theory underscores pivotal elements, which develop the structure and composition of cultural contracts. This is to say that every contract requires a degree of assimilation toward essentialist values and ideals, whether the individual is the composer or the signer of the contract. Of key interest to the researcher is that every contract illustrates signs of essentialism. There are non-negotiable values to which an individual must assimilate in order to be compliant with the cultural contract.

The second of the three-part analysis consists of bringing into fruition the dynamics of cultural contracts and identity negotiation. The researcher will implement Jackson's cultural contract theory. After the contract was negotiated by the characters in *Bamboozled* (2000) and *X* (1992), the characters faced breached contracts. The researcher will explore this quality within the research question.

The research questions are

1. How do Ready-to-sign cultural contracts, Quasi-completed cultural contracts, and Cocreated cultural contracts affect black identity in the films *Bamboozled* (2000) and *X* (1992)?
2. What are the consequences for breaching contracts in the films *Bamboozled* (2000) and *X* (1992)?

Complicity of Negative Difference (*Bamboozled*)
Africa

In the film *Bamboozled* (2000), the essentialist discourse arrives from preexisting racist ideas that whites have about blacks. The racist ideas provide a cultural framework for the way whites would come to understand blacks and their environment. These ideas are communicated in the film *Bamboozled* (2000). In the film *Bamboozled* (2000), Lee depicted Harlem as a destitute place suffused with blacks, who are living in poverty and preoccupied with entertainment. For example, Lee (2000) depicted Manray and Cheeba as unkempt blacks that are social problems for whites. After providing what seems to be a free tap dance show, they hassle people for money.

Cheeba: I'm Cheeba and I introduce to you the world renowned Manray, the man with the educated feet. And as we continue on our world tour, we would like to give you a little somethin', somethin' before you go off to make that money. I give you Manray.
(After Manray stops dancing, the crowd applauds as Cheeba unfolds a brown shopping bag and holds it out in front of them.)

Cheeba: Thank you very much, but please don't go without giving us some cheddar, cheese, money. We prefer twos than fews. I would like to add that both of us are homeless. Not that it means anything.
(A woman is about to dump some change in the brown paper bag.)

Cheeba: I said homeless, ladies and gentlemen. Senorita, do you know what that means?
(Cheeba looks at her and she quickly pulls out a 5-spot from her purse and drops it into the bag.)

On another account, Lee (2000) drew the viewer's attention to Junebug. Junebug is Delacroix's father and a comedian. In one scene, Junebug comments that everyone is good at something. Black people are naturally good at entertaining. Junebug goes on to tell Delacroix that all niggers are entertainers.

The essentialist themes highlighted from Lee's (1992) depiction of Harlem are that Harlem is filled with poverty and that blacks are only prosperous when they are functioning as entertainers. Although these themes are ridiculous, many whites hold these themes as presuppositions of who blacks were/are and what they did/do. Consider, for example, the following dialogue that transpires between Delacroix and Dunwitty. On the wall of Dunwitty's office are prominent blacks. The only problem is that the blacks on the wall are all entertainers. This scene reveals Dunwitty's and many whites' preoccupation with the racist themes mentioned previously:

Dunwitty: Delacroix, wake up, brother man. The reason why [the shows] didn't get picked up was because nobody—and I mean NOBODY—niggers and crackers alike wants to see that junk. ...You know and I know "niggers" set the trend, set the styles.

Delacroix: What is it you want from me? Some *plantation* follies? Some sitcom that takes place on a watermelon patch? Some show that follows *four nigger generations of junkies and crackheads*? You want me to go back to the ante bellum days?

Dunwitty: Yes! Yes! Yes!...

To only think of blacks as entertainers, junkies, and crackheads that live on plantations is a racist logic that is made possible by examining the concept of negative difference. McPhail (1991, 1996a) noted that all language and presuppositions are value-laden, which is to say, language is never neutral. Complicity to negative difference goes beyond language association, or the naming of an idea. Negative difference is adherence to a set of ideological restraints and principles that argue an essential reality.

In short, the examples highlight how essentialist discourse creates a system of racist ideology and negative difference. The researcher points out scenes in which Lee (2002) articulated this type of thinking:

- First, Cheeba and Manray are seen soliciting money. This creates the impression to whites that blacks have a natural propensity for entertainment and begging.
- Second, Delacroix's meeting with Junebug candidly reveals that blacks undisputedly are nothing but entertainers.
- Third, Dunwitty believes that all black people are entertainers, crackheads, and plantation inhabitants.

Cultural Psychological Haven

> Despite the fact that Blacks lived in a social world suffused by White American political, economic, and cultural influences, these Blacks, for the most part, ignored race relations, depicting the Black social world as an isolated universe sustained by happy-go-lucky hedonism. (Washington, 2001, p. 64)

Robert E. Washington (2001) stated, "Harlem was an African oasis, which allowed blacks to transcend the labors and routine of white culture" (p. 80). In short, Lee's (1992) depiction of Harlem was a culturally rich environment that would allow blacks to feel closer to their cultural roots. The following dialogue describes this point.

Mantan: We both left the hustle and bustle of Uptown Harlem...
Sleep 'n Eat: The big apple, New York, New York...
Mantan: To come back to our roots.

38   Analysis

Sleep 'n Eat: Our Alabamy home. Now we're getting countrified. We is Bama's.
Mantan: No mo' "city slickers." Ahh, can't you smell the aroma of the ripe watermelons and cotton?
Sleep 'n Eat: Cousins, first, second, third, and distant, let's have Mantan take us all the way back to a much simpler time. A time when men were men, women were women, and Neggeras knew their place.

The psychological connection to Africa is not to be lost by various geographical locations mentioned in the dialogue but is to be understood by its ideological commentary about the overall character, culture, and nature of the African. In *Bamboozled* (2000), Lee depicted the African as someone who has a simple mind and is avaricious. For example, as Sleep 'n Eat and Mantan are dancing on the stage, they are joined by Jungle Bunny, Snowflake, Sambo, Aunt Jemima, Rastus, and Nigger Jim. These characters are examples of racist stereotypical views of simple-minded and self-indulgent African Americans. Like Mantan and Sleep 'n Eat, the other characters' names are based on racist assumptions. Jungle Bunny, Snowflake, Sambo, Aunt Jemima, Rastus, and Nigger Jim are names that were used to describe blacks. These characters names are names of hate and malice. The names indicate that blacks are lazy, uneducated, and/or overly sexual. Although these characters are just acting, they are communicating an ideology, which is far from benign. McPhail (1991) noted that language projects a reality that people act upon. Throughout the taping, the characters sit on the porch, dance, and eat. Lee's (2000) articulation of these characters suggests that Africans can be satisfied with the simple treatment of eating and sleeping and that the African only flourishes in environments that are slow paced.

Lee's (2000) vision of the characters is essentialist, and the characters are represented as visual ideologies of hate. The characters that Lee (2000) portrayed are not real; however, by being complicit with the ideological portrayal of the characters is to believe that what the characters represent is real. Discourse, within this line of reasoning, is part of a complicit network of ideas that become real because of people's belief in them (McPhail, 1991). Because discourse can seduce people to believe ideas that are not necessarily true, many whites believe that there is an obvious relationship between the characters in the film, black people, and Africans.

Moreover, Lee (2000) depicted the African as somewhat maladaptive in a new environment. This new environment creates anxiety and desire for the African's homeland. The New World, which is the white world, is implied as overly complex and leaves the African in a state of bemusement. The retreat to the south or the north is really a cry for Africa, where life is supposedly simpler. Claude McKay (1928), a literary writer, reported,

> [The] Congo remained in spite of formidable opposition and exploitation. The Congo was real throbbing in little Africa in New York. It was an amusement place entirely for the unwashed of the Black Belt.... The Congo was African in spirit and color. No white persons were admitted. (p. 15)

McKay's (1928) comment is extremely critical because it highlights racist associations that served as the impetus for these outlandish associations. Moreover, since McKay (1928) is black, this comment provides credibility for whites to validate their beliefs and presumptions. The complicit discourse manifests itself in terms of adherence to belief that a monolithic essence exists in black identity. This assumption is based on the principle that difference is not complementary but antagonistic (McPhail, 1996a).

The following points were discussed by McKay (1928):

- The pejorative relationship between Harlem and Africa was based on complicit and hazardous associations that whites had about blacks and Africans.
- Culturally and psychologically, Harlem was a "Garden of Eden," filled with all types of alluring activities; it was exceptionally pleasing for blacks because it supposedly had more similarities to Africa than to the New World (America).

Socioeconomic Conditions

Within the context of negative difference, *Bamboozled* (2000) depicts Harlem as a community victimized with misfortune, fraught with poverty, and populated by African Americans. Most evident of this is Cheeba and Manray's place of residence. In the outskirts of the film, Cheeba and Manray live in an illegal resident building, where living conditions are below code. The only items of any value belonging to Manray and Cheeba are a pair of downtrodden tap shoes and a wooden crate that is used for a stage. Every day, both Cheeba and Manray perform on the street for below-wage earnings just to eat.

Although Cheeba and Manray are homeless and at times without food, their grief and misfortune are seemingly minimal because of their ability to entertain themselves and others by dancing. In other words, entertainment assuages their current state of being. Without analyzing the socioeconomic conditions of poverty and homelessness, the recurring theme resonating is the clueless, unabashed, happy-go-lucky, and poverty-stricken black, whose salvation is entertainment.

By drawing the viewer's attention to an onslaught of coercive images, *Bamboozled* (2000) leaves the viewer with a narrow and limited understanding of the socioeconomic condition of Cheeba and Manray, as well as Harlem. As such, the complicit themes (e.g., clueless, happy-go-lucky, unabashed, poverty stricken) are made possible by race. McPhail (1991) noted that race confronts a reality of negative difference, which calls into question the assumptions that "serious reality" engenders. In short, McPhail's (1996a) assertion of a serious reality is indicative of an essentialist reality. This reality, presented by Lee in *Bamboozled* (2000), shows that blacks are limited in their function to intelligently interact in society. This essentialist reality is also indicative of the group called the Mau-Maus.

Lee (2000) diverted viewers' attention to another musical group in the film, the Mau-Maus. The Mau-Maus are a Black Nationalist urban hip-hop music group who exemplify the same activity and behavior as Cheeba and Manray. Like Cheeba and Manray, the Mau-Maus' primary source of escape is music. In addition to rapping and performing, the Mau-Maus indulge in a variety of illegal drugs. According to Lee (2000), "They pass around joints that look like they've been on steroids and 64-ounce juglars of da bomb malt liquor—liquid crack, the preferred alcoholic beverage of ghetto Negroes."

On the subject of pervasive drug use by African Americans, McKay (1928) remarked that alcohol and cocaine were one of the earliest and cheapest forms of drug use among blacks in Harlem. McKay's (1928) embellished depiction of Harlem and drug use as a commonplace activity represented what he considered to be ordinary black behavior. Both outstanding and incredulous, blacks were not only depicted as hedonistic but also as prodigal and indulgent with no regard for the future.

McKay (1928) and Lee's (2000) examples concerning the prodigal and drug-infected blacks clearly support McPhail's (1991) theory of negative difference. McPhail (1991) noted that if scholars are to examine one set of ideas within a particular symbolic space, that same idea can't occupy the opposite space. In this light, negative difference operates as a set of binary opposites (McPhail, 1991). Consider for example the themes mentioned previously about blacks being clueless, happy-go-lucky, unabashed, and poverty stricken. Within the confines of McPhail's (1991) theory, this means that blacks are not intelligent, wise, without shame, and prosperous. These ideas are communicated throughout the film and in the dialogues that follow.

Tavis Smiley: Let's jump right into it. Your show has sparked a world of controversy, provoked a tone of dialogue. How do you see all of this?

Mantan: Yo, Tavis, check it out. This is the two-one, the 21st century, and it's all about the money. Like my man Mase says, "It's all about the Benjamins."
Tavis Smiley: Money and nothing else?
Mantan: Money makes the world go round.

When Mantan mentions, "Its all about the Benjamins," he is communicating a reckless type of thinking that leads to wasteful spending habits and careless behavior. Early in the film, Mantan communicates to Cheeba that the first thing he is going to do when he makes it is "buy a car with some nice rims" (Lee, 2002). Cheeba agrees, "I want the Hill-Nigga set up" (Lee, 2002). The point is that when the two actors "made it," that is exactly what they did. Cheeba and Manray spend their money on goods that have temporal and no sustaining monetary value. Not limited to socioeconomic mobility, *Bamboozled* (2000) makes the claim that both the lower-class and upper-class blacks are susceptible to gluttony, demonstrating impatience and extravagance (Lucia, 2001).

Consider, for example, the character Pierre Delacroix, who represents one of the few African Americans who is successful. Delacroix has a Harvard education, dresses professionally, is very well spoken, and holds a major position at the television station. Although Delacroix doesn't dress in expensive urban attire, he wears expensive suits and watches and has an excessive amount of living space that he barely can afford. The following statement by Dunwitty testifies to these ideas.

Dunwitty: You got your head stuck up your ass with your Harvard education and your pretentious ways.

Dunwitty's comment exploits Delacroix's relentless effort to assimilate into the white culture. In his attempt to assimilate, he buys the house, goes to the right schools, speaks the right language, and even changes his birth name (Pierless to Pierre). According to Tondeur (2001), in Dunwitty's mind, Delacroix is an "oreo." Stuart Hall reported, "Symbolic lines are being drawn, and what we know about culture is that once the symbolic difference exists…power uses difference as a way of marking off who does and who does not belong" (Lubiano, 1998, p. 298). Delacroix will buy and do anything to persuade others that he is not black. In support of this idea, Dunwitty comments on Delacroix's pretentious persona:

Dunwitty: Brother man, I'm blacker than you. I'm keeping it real, and you're frontin', trying to be white.
Delacroix: I'm an oreo, a sell out? Because I don't aspire to do Homeboys from Outer Space…[or] some "nigger" show? I'm a Tom? I'm whiter than white and you're blacker than black? Is that what you think?

Dunwitty: That's exactly what I think.

(In a different scene, Delacroix comes into a board meeting late.)

Dunwitty: Do you know how much information can be dispensed in one minute alone?

Delacroix: I didn't find out about this very important staff meeting until.... (Delacroix rolls up his sleeve, looking at his Jaeger-LeCoultre.)

In the subsequent scene, Delacroix comments that he would have canceled his Pilots session if he had been aware of the meeting. What is of importance in this situation has nothing to do with his coming to the meeting late or that he wasn't informed of the meeting, but has everything to do with the artifacts and lifestyle that symbolize his quest for upward social mobility. Rogin (2001) stated that Delacroix, although educated, will embrace any artifact that outwardly communicates how dapper and well-to-do he is. Nonetheless, Delacroix is depicted as the stereotypical black who is frivolous and excessive.

Truly, there is little difference between Delacroix's character and any other black who the researcher examines in the film. Yes, these characters are in different social and economic situations but they all are frivolous and excessive. In addition, the commitment to Lee's (2000) description of the characters as virtually the same can be understood through negative difference. McPhail (1996b) noted that a significant component of negative difference is epistemological foundationalism. Epistemological foundationalism, like essentialism, claims that there is a reality in which material and symbolic processes exist in and of themselves, in which they are justified either on the basis of belief in some externally validated, reliably referenced reality that is aimed at the discovery of essential truths. To this end, Lee (2000) depicted Cheeba, Manray, and Delacroix as virtually the same. Moreover, epistemological foundationalism is the impetus for these essentialist assumptions.

To close this section of analysis, *Bamboozled* (2000) purports that complicity of negative difference makes possible the essentialist proclamations and associations concerning blacks, Harlem, and their socioeconomic position. The following points have been discussed:

- The major premise is that Harlem is based on epistemological foundationalism and a crude relationship that is thought to be indicative of Africa. Complicity of negative difference enunciates this crude relationship through three categories: Africa, cultural psychological, and Socioeconomic Conditions. The researcher's argument supports the premise that Harlem, like Africa, is depicted as simple and uncomplicated. To this end, activities such as dancing, prodigal behavior, and sport require little to no adaptation for blacks.

- The second premise set forth is supported by the prodigal behavior of Delacroix, Cheeba, Manray, and the Mau-Maus. Each character displays a different type of frivolous behavior and thinking pattern. Wilson (1999) noted that these behaviors have been underscored as essentialist and natural character traits of the African American.

Complicity of Negative Difference (*X*)

Africa

Harlem and Africa signify a provocative relationship in the film *X* (1992). The relationship between Harlem and Africa is best understood through negative difference; this specific perspective allows for a scrupulous deconstruction of the racist relationship articulated by Lee (1992).

Lee's vision of Harlem in the film *X* (1992) was based on the actual Harlem Renaissance, which started in the 1920s and ended in 1930. From this perspective, the discourse that resonates from Lee's articulation of the actual Harlem Renaissance is complicit and limited. Lee (1992) acknowledged and privileged some ideas about Harlem, while ignoring and marginalizing others. Harlem, in Lee's (1992) eyes, may have been downtrodden, and the blacks in Harlem may have been prodigal, gluttonous, sordid, and so forth, but this was only Lee's interpretation. In this light, Lee (1992) was complicit. McPhail (1996a) noted, "This is the phenomenon of complicity, and it is rooted in the tendency of critical discourse to privilege itself even as it calls privilege into question" (p. 69).

From Lee's perspective in *X* (1992), blacks had an affinity to Harlem that was quite mystical. In the film, when Malcolm is riding the train to Harlem, there is a song playing in the background, "Take Me Home to Harlem." As Malcolm steps off the train smiling, thousands of blacks crowd into the streets to cheer the recent victory of Joe Lewis' boxing match. The song playing in the background is a rhetorical strategy to emphasize the importance of Harlem to blacks. Analogously, Harlem can be likened to the Holy city Mecca, a bastion of hope and salvation for African Americans.

Because negative difference allows individuals to limit or expand their comprehension of ideas, by claiming they have an essence, individuals' ability to experience these ideas can be either truncated or augmented (McPhail, 1996b). In the film *X* (1992), the Harlem Renaissance of the 1920s–1930s is nothing short of heaven; blacks from all over the country aspired to be in Harlem. By understanding Harlem through essentialist terms, Lee's (2002) depiction of the Harlem Renaissance of the 1920s–1930s was more attractive because of its idealistic qualities than its geographical location or social problems. McPhail (1996a) noted "This is what happens when discourse seduces itself; the original way in which discourse absorbs meaning empties itself of meaning in order to fascinate others" (p. 96). In short, Harlem, a geographical location, was transformed into something more. No longer was it understood for its physical qualities or social and racial issues; rather, Harlem was understood for its utopian qualities. The following paragraphs are examples of negative difference, which resonate from Lee's (1992) vision of Harlem and the blacks that occupy Harlem. They are examples of negative difference; they claim that there exists an essential and foundationalist reality that can be found in Harlem and in blacks. In addition, they are complicit in that they highlight specific notions of Harlem and blacks, while ignoring others.

The first articulation of Harlem in the film *X* (1992) takes place in the downtown business district. Lee drew the viewer's attention to blacks doing meager and illegal jobs for minimal wage, from shining shoes, to carrying groceries, to peddling merchandise and prostituting. Because of the racism that persisted in the 1920s, blacks had few or no options for employment and livelihood. As such, blacks had to feverishly search for employment and take jobs with salaries below minimum wage. Subsequently, Lee depicted these same blacks spending their minimum wage dollars at dance clubs and trendy bars. Unfittingly, the complicit ideology begins to evolve: these back-to-back episodes depict Harlem as destitute and blacks as needy and socially maladaptive, Harlem as a place where blacks could retire from the daily labors of life and spend the little they had with no regard for the future. Or, instead of searching for a well-paying job, blacks could resort to fantasizing about the future while playing children's games to take their mind off their problems.

Consider, for example, Malcolm and Shorty running in the park, jumping on occupied benches, rolling in the leaves, playing cops and robbers, and using their hands for guns; they both were adults who were acting juvenile and immature. The relationship suggested in the film again reinforces the idea that blacks are disruptive and that Harlem is the unruly area they fit in. In support of this argument and the example above, Malcolm states that he is scared of three things: "job, bust, and jail." These were facts of life that Malcolm did not have to face outside of Harlem. As long as he stayed with his people and did not intermingle with whites, he did not have to worry about a job, bust, or jail.

The young Malcolm, like many blacks who have faced extreme hardships, found it difficult to do the right thing because the social system did little to support him or aid him in getting out of his depraved condition. To this end, unsavory activity at least provides some blacks with a fighting chance to disconnect from their ominous state and become positive contributors to society and, in doing so, not fall victim to jail, a meager job, or a bust. The point is X (1992) depicted Harlem as different from white culture; it was a culture saturated with black worldviews. According to Lee (1992), Harlem had its own distinct rules, language, and values, with moderate white influence.

Outside of Harlem, blacks had to assimilate to a Eurocentric model of social appropriateness. The distinct polarity between Harlem (black culture) and white culture, and failure to appreciate cultural differences for what they are, created racial tension for many whites and blacks in the film. As a defense mechanism, many whites conjured stereotypes and racist narratives to veil their own lack of understanding and deficiencies.

X's (1992) commitment to Harlem and Africa as primitive and immoral is also evident in the social relationships that transpire between Malcolm and Shorty, Malcolm and Sophia, and Malcolm's involvement with West Indian Archie. These relationships all are questionable and opportunistic; they are based on illegal activity or immoral behavior and cost and reward and are devoid of any altruism. More important, the relationships take place in an environment that supports such a relationship (e.g., Harlem). Malcolm's relationship with both Shorty and West Indian Archie centers around drug activity, hustling, and stealing. Malcolm's relationship with Sophia centers on the same type of activity, but it is also inclusive of a prohibited interracial relationship.

Locke (1925) submitted, southerners and northerners alike shared a commitment to stereotype blacks as buffoons and degenerates, or at best as subservient lackeys with juvenile and irresponsible behavior. Rhonda Williams (Lubiano, 1998) stated,

> Western racist discourses routinely construct "Blackness" as a problematic sign and ontological position. In doing so, the architects of cultural and (social) scientific racism historically have represented Black communities, Black families, and Black bodies as the bearers of stigma, disease, danger, violence, social pathology, and hypersexuality. (p. 140)

In short, X (1992) suggests that Harlem and Africa are based on the theory of negative difference that is marked by essentialism and foundationalism. Negative difference is a two-edged sword. Harlem for the blacks was a mystical icon, a place of harbor and safety. Just the same, negative difference explains how white racist discourse is used to denigrate and support the pejorative and essentialist suppositions about blacks.

On the basis of Lee's (1992) reconstruction of the Harlem Renaissance, negative difference manifests in connections between Lee's re-

construction of the Harlem Renaissance and the actual Harlem. According to Lee (1992), Harlem was more of an ideal than a geographic location. Harlem was suffused with all types of cultural artifacts and atmosphere, which made it attractive.
- Although Lee (1992) depicted various examples of Harlem's mystical appeal, Lee (1992) also articulated Harlem as culture filled with plenty of societal problems. Lee (1992) never bothers to provide an explanation of these problems, leaving the viewer with a pejorative image of Harlem.
- In the film *X* (1992), Harlem is an immoral counterculture. Harlem, unlike other places, makes way for a large array of illegal activity. In *X* (1992), Lee directs viewers' attention to prohibited interracial relationships, drug-related activity, and prostitution. Although these ideas may not seem uncommon, the manner in which Lee (1992) presents these issues as a black problem, as if no other community has such issues, is of significance.

Cultural Psychological Haven

X (1992) depicts the African in Harlem as temperamental and naïve. Lee (1992) explored negative difference by investigating the relationship blacks had with Harlem. *X* (1992) makes this case by exploring the psychological framework that most blacks seemed to have. Lee (1992) depicted these frameworks as symbolic and ideological codes of language, which share in a racist rhetorical vision of self-hate. To this end, blacks are viewed as individuals who are desperately seeking a way out of their condition, by adopting a discourse of self-hate. McPhail (1996b) noted, "We are taking language, not as a system of abstract grammatical categories, but rather language conceived as ideologically saturated, language as a worldview, even as concrete opinion" (p. 80).

The successful black was one who looked furthest from being black; in divorcing from his or her culture, the successful black would do anything to look apart. The same stood true for Malcolm. Malcolm, in the film, is seen getting lye applied to his scalp. After Malcolm is treated with lye, he gingerly touches his hair; smiling, he says, "Looks white." Harlem came to psychologically signify the reservoir of possibilities for African-American pride. Blacks could fantasize about white privilege and power within an insulated environment (e.g., Harlem). McPhail (1996a) stated that being complicit to negative difference is not choosing when or where to negotiate thinking patterns; it is to buy into a whole network of logocentric thinking. Complicity in *X* (1992) is then the playing out of white cultural fantasies and the debasing of black cultural beliefs for white systems of ideology and beliefs. Through negative difference, evidence of complicit thinking claims begins to surface.

In the film *X* (1992), characters such as Malcolm, Shorty, and West Indian Archie engage in an opportunity to exercise their fantasies and desires, reconfirming essentialist claims about blacks. Shorty and West Indian Archie straighten their hair to look white. Shorty and Malcolm aspire after white women. Lee (1992) ostracized these characters as examples of blacks aspiring to be white. Even more, this attitude is indicative of some blacks that live and frequent Harlem. Specifically, blacks managed to create an oppressive and racist system, based on color and essentialist discourse. For those blacks living in Harlem, being complicit to white cultural patterns was a way to increase social, political, and economic mobility; this type of behavior requires one to buy into a system of negative difference in which one culture is recognized and the other is ignored (McPhail, 1996b).

The oppressive and racist system consisted of a middle class and a lower class. Those characterized as middle class were admitted to the most prestigious social organizations and enjoyed certain economic advantages over their black counterparts, who were of a lower class and of darker skin hue. The lower class were excluded from certain social organizations because of their meager jobs and other ill-defined attributes. The point being made is that Harlem represented not only an insulated environment for the black person, but it was also a place where blacks could explore their fantasies about privilege and whiteness. Most important, Lee (1992) validated and championed white culture, while communicating a level of disdain for black culture. Emerging this juxtaposition of discourse is a very clear but erroneous reality.

> Our perceptions of reality are intimately connected to the way we construct the world with words, and much of what we have constructed, at least in terms of what we believe to be real, is at best an illusion and at worst a delusion. And the most dangerous illusion of all is that there is only one reality. (McPhail, 1996a, p. 104)

In addition to promoting an essentialist reality, one to which some blacks would have gravitated, many blacks in the film developed an identity crisis (Lee, 1992). To this end, Lee (1992) depicted Harlem as the seaport for identity crisis. The black was an individual who was caught between the recognition that he or she was a person of color and that he or she could negotiate his or her blackness in Harlem. Between both dichotomies and realizations, blacks were faced with an identity issue. This issue of identity is often dubbed "double-consciousness." Du Bois (1903) articulated that the "double-consciousness" is a result of the inherent struggle of being both black and an American. In the film *X* (1992), the black in Harlem was made aware of his or her authentic dilemma. Blacks were ostracized by their own people, or they were ostracized by the mainstream culture (Wilson, 1999). McPhail (1996a) noted that oppositional discourse by default makes one realize negative difference; it is a discourse in which one is made aware of essentialism by virtue of his or her heterogeneity. McPhail (1991) attributed oppositional discourse and negative difference as a cultural pattern invested in language. "This belief in separateness has, indeed, made us strangers, and has created a language of negative difference which manifests itself in the social and symbolic spaces of race, gender and rhetoric" (McPhail, 1996b, p. 66). Up until Malcolm's prison years, Lee (1992) depicted the black person as confused and disconnected from his or her culture. Lee (1992) illustrated this dilemma by directing the viewer's attention to Malcolm's choices in women and Malcolm's own self-concept about blackness.

When choosing whom to date, Malcolm chooses Sophia (a white woman) over Laura (a black woman). Reasons for this can be traced to Malcolm's tumultuous feelings concerning whiteness and blackness. Illustrations of this internal conflict are evident in three situations from the film.

In the first situation, Malcolm rushes to take Laura home, only to return to the dance in hopes of developing a relationship with Sophia. Malcolm feels that a relationship with Sophia is more beneficial than one with Laura because Sophia is white, not religious, and willing to have sexual relations. Malcolm's behavior suggests a complicity in believing that white is better. This idea is what propels Malcolm to pursue a relationship with Sophia. Whiteness for Malcolm was a symbol of purity, as the following dialogue shows.

Malcolm: So I will call you tomorrow in the morning.
Laura: What for? I'm not white and I don't put out, so why would you want to call me, Malcolm?

Sophia: Am I the first white woman you been with?
Malcolm: No, I had plenty!
Sophia: That's not a whore?

The questions asked by Sophia are significant. If Malcolm is to believe that white women are a prize, then Sophia makes it clear that not just any white woman is a prize. A prostitute doesn't count, but a woman of respect and integrity counts.

In a later scene, after Malcolm is thrown into jail, he is befriended by Brother Bains, a Muslim. Brother Bains witnesses to Malcolm about his ways and warns him about his foolish behavior. While Malcolm is in the shower room washing the lye out of his hair, Brother Bains approaches him.

Bains: Look at you, puttin' all that poison in your hair.

Malcolm: I think you been in prison too long, my man, because everyone on the outside conks.
Bains: Why? Why does everyone on the outside conk?
Malcolm: Because they don't want to walk around with a nappy hair lookin' like...
Bains: Lookin like what? Like me? Like a Nigga? Why don't you want to look like what you are? What makes you ashamed of being black?
Malcolm: I'm not ashamed of being black.
(Malcolm turns to wash the conk out of his hair. Bains then grabs his arm.)
Bains: Let it burn.
Malcolm: Get your hands off me.
Bains: Go on burn yourself, pain yourself, put all that poison in your hair and in your body, trying to be white. I thought you were smart. You are just another cat struttin' in your clown suits with all that mess in ya, lookin' like a monkey. The white man sees ya and laughs. He laughs because he knows you're not white.
Malcolm: Who are you?
Bains: No, the question is who are you?

These scenes depict a conflict that was not just typical of Malcolm, but many black men who aspired to be white. The mindset of the black was such that whiteness was better than blackness. In the first scene, Malcolm and Sophia talk about whiteness as if it were a prize or something to be desired. In the subsequent dialogue, Bains and Malcolm have an intense argument about whiteness, blackness, and identity. Key in this dialogue is Bains' assertion that Malcolm doesn't want to look like a "Nigga." Bains' statement speaks to the fact that many blacks, like Malcolm, masquerade as if they are white, testifying that they are ashamed of their identity. Bains' question, "No, the question is who are you?" addresses Malcolm's dilemma with his own identity. McPhail (1991) suggested that once systems of negative difference have been internalized, they create categories of value that construct a universe of alternate meanings. A term, which is harmless and innocent, can be manipulated to be pejorative and harmful, creating levels of xenophobia. Lee (1992) illustrated this idea through Malcolm's quagmire.

- First, according to Lee (1992), Malcolm, like some of the blacks in Harlem, was persuaded into a complicit way of thinking about black culture. Creating a level of self-hate, some blacks valorized white culture, while shunning black culture.
- The second premise and argument set forth is that black self-hate created an ideological system of oppression, one that was based on color

complexion and class. To this end, blacks that were of a lighter hue and in the right organizations were ultimately treated better.
- Third, the number of blacks who chose to assimilate into a discourse of complicity experienced an identity crisis. Torn between their identity and the ability to negotiate their identity, many blacks experienced a loss of self, as is indicated in the dialogue between Bains and Malcolm.

Socioeconomic Conditions

Like Africa, Harlem in the film *X* (1992) was fecund with many resources. Blacks from various parts of the United States migrated to experience Harlem in its glory. The migration was due to the North's liberal reputation and the living conditions, which were better than the South's. During the 1920s, the migration of blacks into upper Manhattan helped to provide the ideological and material resources to launch the artistic explosion known as the Harlem Renaissance (Washington, 2001). Moreover, Lee's (1992) reconstruction of Harlem presented a turbulent and thorny array of illegal activity, politics, religion, and art that fueled various aspects of the Harlem dream. To this end, what Harlem came to signify really isn't clear, but there were huge migrations into Harlem.

The cost of living increased as blacks and whites migrated to Harlem. With fewer legitimate jobs available, illegal activities became a more commonplace means of raising capital. For example, the dialogue between the bartender and Malcolm concerning West Indian Archie attests to some of this environmental distress.

>(Malcolm orders a single shot of whisky from the bartender. By order of Archie, the bartender gives Malcolm a double.)

Malcolm: I ordered a single "Jack."
Bartender: The order is on that gentleman "Jack."
Malcolm: Who's that?
Bartender: That's West Indian Archie.
Malcolm: Yeah, what's his angle?
Bartender: Some of this and some of that.

X (1992) depicts African Americans as shrewd hustlers driven by their own understanding of success, even if it means hurting others. Archie, for example, is both a drug dealer and bookie and operates myriad illegal operations. These illegal operations are lucrative, yet they perpetuate an essentialist worldview of African-American culture. In no way do Archie's operations contribute to a restorative African-American ethos. In all cases, the operations communicate a discourse of complicity, which proclaims that black and illegal activities are one in the same.

The discourse is complicit in that it suggests that blacks are a problem, the burden that holds society down and keeps society from reaching its potential. Although this is furthest from the truth, X (1992) presents this illusion as real. These assumptions and illusions are based on erroneous essentialist and foundationalist ideas. Because the concept of blackness is not based on foundationalism and essentialism, it is not easily conceptualized. Blackness, or the concept of black, is dynamic, and because blackness is dynamic it is always changing. McPhail (1996a) noted that essentialism and foundationalism are based on the idea that every term has an essence or at least can be understood by certain qualities. Since a term such as "blackness" or "black" rejects both essentialism and foundationalism, it is easier to capriciously group black people in the film X (1992) with a series of ideas than it is to work through the various layers of meaning.

Another part of the socioeconomic culture that contributes to the Harlem dream is religion. After Malcolm yields to the Nation of Islam, he, like other converted religious speakers, speaks on the street corners of Harlem. Lee (1992) portrayed speakers such as Malcolm, Reverend Al Sharpton, and other prominent black orators, jockeying for the attention of streetwalkers. More important than the speakers was the informal congregation of blacks around the podium. These people looked needy and ready to grasp on to the message in order to make them feel good about themselves. Religion for blacks is especially important because it is a safe release from the trenches of racial oppression and menial living. Religion promised solace and comfort in times of distress (Asante, 2002). As Malcolm testifies to the black women in X (1992),

> You do not have to earn a living caring for whites' houses, washing their clothes, and caring for their children. You don't have to stand outside begging for a job. They are looking at you, and examining you, like you are some type of slave. You are black and you're beautiful.

X (1992) examines African Americans as unsophisticated. In the previous passage, Lee (1992) depicted blacks as overly irrational because of their dedication to religion and religion as an escape. Although religion can boost one's self-esteem, in no way should it be berated to something, which appears to be a narcotic. The previous passage is evidence of this claim. The main point in both examples is to illustrate the various essentialist worldviews that are made possible by crude associations (Lee, 1992).

The preceding paragraphs provide several examples that illustrate the socioeconomic conditions that blacks confronted:

- Specifically, the complicit mystiques that were associated with Harlem were the impetus for the migration to Harlem. To this end, Harlem was a series of nebulous ideologies rather than a geographical location.
- Thwarting the hopes and wishes of blacks were the stark realities of life. Consequently, some blacks retreated to illegal activities in order to maintain economic equilibrium. To this end, black and illegal activity became one in the same.
- Religion served as an innocuous, but effective, discourse, counteracting the pains of psychological oppression for blacks. The essentialist argument is that although blacks felt most at ease when they were enveloped by securities of religion, religion was a fixed and stable entity that never yielded to societal attitudes and ideological shifts. To this end, Lee (1992) presented blacks as religious junkies.

Contract Theory—Analysis I (*Bamboozled*)

The rhetorical dimension of contract theory illustrates the in-depth relationship between identity and the negotiation process within a communicative context. The communicative context analyzed is understood as a cultural contract. Cultural contracts explicate the inextricable and symbiotic relationship between a person's identity and various communicative interactions that affect his or her identity.

The ideas to follow examine several things. First, the ideas examine the rhetorical dimensions that impel the characters toward negotiation. Second, the ideas conceptualize the rhetorical conditions, which identify the ideas as the contract(s) of negotiation.

The analysis of *Bamboozled* (2000) and *X* (1992) unfolds in the following order. *Bamboozled* is the first in the order of two films analyzed, then *X*. The first contract that is explored is a Ready-to-sign cultural contract. The characters involved are Manray and Cheeba. The second contract analyzed is that of Pierre Delacroix. The contract assigned to him is also a Ready-to-sign cultural contract. In the film *Bamboozled* (2000), there are times when the characters' names change. This is due to a change in identity. The following changes will occur at various times in the study: Manray to Mantan, and Cheeba to Sleep 'n Eat.

Following the study of *Bamboozled* (2000) is the film *X* (1992). The character analyzed in this film is Malcolm X. The contracts which best illustrate the negotiation process for Malcolm are Quasi-completed cultural contract, Ready-to-sign cultural contract, and Cocreated cultural contract. In all, the effort to highlight contractual and identity relations makes way for the researcher to answer the following research questions, which appear in the third segment:

Analysis 53

1. How do Ready-to-sign cultural contracts, Quasi-completed cultural contracts, and Cocreated cultural contracts affect black identity in the films *Bamboozled* (2002) and *X* (1992)?
2. What are the consequences for breaching contracts in the films *Bamboozled* (2000) and *X* (1992)?

Ready-to-Sign Cultural Contract (A)

From the time the film commences until it ends, both Manray and Cheeba are depicted as psychologically unbalanced characters. Torn between the stark reality of their economic and social condition, the characters are impelled by societal pressures to assimilate and by doing so escape their abject situation. In a voice-over, Lee (2000) described both Manray and Cheeba's living situation as destitute:

> The tenant building is boarded up, condemned, bombed out, but a home, a shelter nonetheless. People, to our surprise, live here. It is a commune: the homeless, people who have been left out, forgot about, written off, don't matter; the fringes of society.

Other examples of Manray and Cheeba's condition include their deficiency in basic hygiene and social appropriateness. Delacroix and Sloan confirm between themselves that before the tandem perform, or are given a cash advancement, there should be certain social standards of appropriateness that must be met. Said in another way, Manray and Cheeba must totally negotiate their identity. Delacroix and Sloan feel the social disparity and inadequacy separating them from Manray and Cheeba. This disparity insinuates that Delacroix and Sloan are better than Manray and Cheeba because they are more coached and socially competent. The division among the two sets of characters can be understood through Llorens' (1968) fable.

Llorens (1968) described two types of blacks: the fellow and the chosen one. The fellow (e.g., Manray and Cheeba) is familiar with the streets, knows the latest vernacular, and is unabashed because he or she is being "real." Contrary to the fellow is the chosen one (e.g., Delacroix and Sloan). These individuals are similar to those who surmount their current depraved situation to be culturally refined. These individuals are embarrassed, feel a level of discomfort when the fellow is around, and fear that they may say or do something that indicts the whole race. Through the eyes of Delacroix and Sloan, Manray and Cheeba are likened to the "primitive African" and share similar character traits (e.g., uncouth, inappropriate, naïve, desperate). By examining the two different sets of characters through the fable, the ideological small print within the contract becomes larger.

Beyond the physical yearnings to look alike or to fit in, Manray and Cheeba desire to be accepted by mainstream culture and to have access to many of the pleasures that the mainstream culture enjoys. West (1993) assessed the dilemma as a quest for blacks to seek approbation from whites, a neurosis "that seems to lock Black people into the quest for White approval" (p. 139). According to Du Bois (1903),

> The Negro is a sort of seventh son, born with a veil, and gifted with second-sight in this American world, a world which yields him no true self-consciousness, but only lets him see himself through the revelation of the other world. It is a peculiar sensation, this double-consciousness, this sense of always looking at one's self through the eyes of others, of measuring one's soul by the tape of a world that looks on in amused contempt and pity. (p. 3)

Enticed by pictures of success, Manray and Cheeba enrapture themselves in pleasures such as Tommy Hillnigger, rims, jewelry, cars, and other symbolic materials. These were the prerequisites that Manray and Cheeba needed to feel accepted and to be one of "them." Manray defends this philosophy in the following passage.

Manray: Money makes the world go round. It ain't no joke being poor. I know what I'm talkin' 'bout. Y' know what I'm sayin'? I've lived on the street. I've been homeless. I've learned how to play the game, work the game, be in the game.

This statement captures two important points: it highlights the mindset of both characters, and it examines success as a game (a series of wins or losses), an onslaught of achievements, that is impelled by money. A major danger in examining one's value in terms of incongruous criteria is an inescapable and never-ending tussle. West (1993) stated, "The modern Black diasporan problematic of invisibility and namelessness can be understood as the condition of relative lack of Black power to represent themselves to themselves and others as complex human beings" (p. 16). This description of the self characterizes the self as vacant and void. In other words, the self lacks the ability to represent itself or to make itself known; being that it no longer can support itself, it collapses. The remnants left behind are disorder and chaos. Both characters find themselves in this sea of chaos and entropy.

The examples tell a poignant narrative about the rhetorical conditions that envelop the characters. These conditions are necessary, leading to the development of a Ready-to-sign cultural contract. Jackson (2002) reported, "Cultural contracts are pre-negotiated and no further negotiation is allowed" (p. 48). More to the point, the contract implies total assimilation and surrendering of one's identity. According to

Jackson (2002), the contract implies that a working relationship is not interactional and that total compliance must be met in order for the contract to be successful.

The contract ascribed to Cheeba and Manray is that of a Ready-to-sign cultural contract. Mentioned in the preceding paragraphs, societal conditions made any contract enticing. The social conditions were so abject that both characters' bargaining power was at a minimum. The contract in which one is involved reveals one's relational position within the communicative dynamic. This aspect is important because it reveals the dynamics of power, the conditions in which power will operate, and who will benefit from the power. Cheeba and Manray were the one's who signed the contract as opposed to drafting the contract. The consequences of this are daunting, as the following conversation indicates:

Cheeba: Manray needs a job.
Manray: We got evicted from our home. We've both been on the streets for the last week.
Delacroix: I have a concept for a TV pilot. There's no guarantee it will get made, but regardless, you'll still make some money.
Cheeba: How much?
Delacroix: First things first. I have to know if Manray is up for this.
Manray: What do I have to do?
Delacroix: Some tap dancing, some singing.
Manray: Where do I sign?
Cheeba: What kind of show is this gonna be?
Delacroix: Different.
Manray: How different?
Delacroix: Trust me. Of course, I still have to pitch it to my boss, but we'll have an answer one way or the other.
Manray: *DeLa, I'm aboard. As long as I get to hoof and get paid, too.*
Delacroix: *I would like to change your name.*
Manray: To what?
Delacroix: *You're now Mantan.*
Manray: *Mantan? I don't even care as long as I'm dancing. Which reminds me, I need some new kicks.*

After Delacroix shows Manray his character (Mantan) on an old television episode, a more compelling dialogue follows.

Delacroix: I want to start using the name *Mantan* and not *Manray* if you don't mind.
Manray: Why?

Delacroix: You have to start getting into your character.
(Delacroix shows Mantan Moreland on television.)
Cheeba: That ain't funny.
Manray: I don't know 'bout this.
Delacroix: Gentleman, the show, our show will be satirical. You know what that is, don't you? Trust me on this one.
Cheeba: We might need some mo' money behind this.
Delacroix: That can be done.

Evident from this dialogue is that Delacroix is the composer of the contract, and the individuals signing the contract are Cheeba and Manray. What strikes the researcher as interesting is Delacroix's requests to change Manray's name from Manray to Mantan; this strategy is ideologically driven, playing a critical and necessary step in the negotiation process. In later dialogue, Dunwitty changes Cheeba's name to Sleep 'n Eat. Names are important, for they are a person's first introduction to the nebulous concept of identity and self. In the absence of a name, the foundation of one's identity is destabilized. A name provides fortitude and direction in a chaotic and uncalculated world. The consequences of an individual without an identity should be self-evident.

> A further substantive question about ideology is what features or levels of language discourse may be ideologically invested. A common claim is that it is 'meanings' that are ideological (e.g., Thompson, 1984), and this often means just or mainly lexical meanings. Lexical meanings are of course important, but so too are presuppositions, implicatures, metaphors, and coherence, all, aspects of meaning. (Fairclough, 1992, p. 74)

It is not satisfactory to examine Delacroix's act as a simple process of name swapping; the revamping of Cheeba and Manray's names creates a new frame of reference in which to examine the characters.

Language is not just a remote tool to communicate facts. Language is emotive; it communicates individuals' relationship with the world. More important, language reveals personal attitudes, values, beliefs, and other ideological/political orientations. Manray and Sleep 'n Eat as new names are both examples of this idea. Both Mantan and Sleep 'n Eat's names are politically and racially loaded; they historically communicate pre-existing and existing sentiment about African Americans. Fairclough (1992) stated that every aspect of discourse may be ideologically significant. As such, names are viewed as ideological portraits that are set and hinged by denotative statements. From this point forward, the Ready-to sign contract is both set and ready to carry out its purpose.

The contract satisfied both the necessary and sufficient conditions enacted by Delacroix. Because of Cheeba and Manray's demeanor, Delacroix made significant value judgments about the conditions in which they would work with them. These judgments were highly symbolic, dictating a language of essentialist ideology that would dominate all communication thereafter. Specifically, these essentialist templates would influence how the two would be treated, how they would be perceived, and ultimately, their fate as African Americans.

Because communication is interactional and often understood through assumptions, Cheeba and Manray understand Delacroix's role in the television station on the basis of his outward appearance. Cheeba and Manray see Delacroix's stature (e.g., chosen one) nothing short of superior. This is due to Delacroix's fancy suits and use of language, money, and power, which have little to do with Delacroix's true function at the television station. These essentialist and hypnotic qualities make both Cheeba and Manray star struck, which makes the assimilation process less coarse. As such, both characters acquiesce to the power dynamic set by Delacroix. It is no mistake that the rhetorical and power dynamic enforced is asymmetrical, benefiting Delacroix.

By and large, the Ready-to-sign cultural contract serves as the template for the communicative interaction thereafter. The dialogue among Cheeba, Manray, and Delacroix provides fruitful examples, illustrating the asymmetrical power dynamics (on the basis of essentialism) in the contract. The contract becomes actualized in the meeting between Mr. Dunwitty (the television producer), Delacroix, and Sloan.

Sloan: Mr. Dunwitty, there wouldn't be another show like it.
Cheeba: I always wanted to be on television.
Dunwitty: I like you, *Sleep 'n Eat*. That's funny. How do you feel about performing in blackface?
Sleep 'n Eat: As long as the hoofing is real, that I can do my thing, I can blacken up.

Dunwitty transforms Cheeba into a character named *Sleep 'n Eat*. Similar to Mantan's dilemma, so to speak, both characters are psychologically forlorn with scrambled identities. The breaking down of the character's core identity is substituted with a frail and hollow identity. Moreover, the collapse of identity makes way for a social state of entropy and bewilderment for the characters. The ideological dimension of this example points to the socio-political struggle between hegemonic interests and society.

> Hegemony is a focus of constant struggle around points of greatest instability between classes and blocs, to construct or sustain or fracture alliances and relations of domination/subordination, which takes

economic, political and ideological forms. Hegemonic struggle takes place on a broad front which includes the institutions of civil society (education, trade unions, family [self concept]). (Fairclough, 1992, p. 76)

Ready-to-Sign Cultural Contract (B)

In the opening moments of the film, Delacroix exemplifies qualities of a well-educated individual who graduated from Harvard, dresses in the most lavish clothes, owns a penthouse in the center of Manhattan, and has a very respectable position in the broadcast agency. Moreover, the opening scenes depict Delacroix's willingness to separate himself from other African Americans. This aspect is critical because it foreshadows Delacroix's contract, the Ready-to-sign cultural contract. The following dialogue is an example of Delacroix's contract.

Dunwitty: You got your head stuck up your ass with your Harvard education and your pretentious ways. Brother man,…I'm keeping it real and you're frontin', trying to be white.

Delacroix: I'm an oreo? A sell out? Because I don't aspire to do Homeboys from Outer Space, Secret Diary of Desmond Pfeiffer, a PJ's or as some of you might put it, some "nigger" show? I'm a Tom? I'm whiter than white and you're blacker than black? Is that what you think?

Dunwitty: That's exactly what I think. I want you to create something that people want to see. Let's be honest, the majority of the people in this country are deaf, dumb, and blind, and I'm including 35 million African Americans.

Delacroix: *I'm not sure if I can deliver what you want.*

Dunwitty: *You will or you'll be back at BET so quick you'll never know what hit you.*

Delacroix: What is it you want from me? Some plantation follies? Some sitcom that takes place on a watermelon patch? Some show that follows four nigger generations of junkies and crackheads? You want me to go back to the ante bellum days?

Dunwitty: Yes! Yes! Yes! I want a show that will make headlines…I'm gonna squeeze this show out of you even if it kills you.

The dialogue between Dunwitty and Delacroix is significant, clearly and candidly explicating the conditions in which Delacroix will operate. To reiterate a point, Ready-to-sign cultural contracts are contracts in which there are no negotiations because they are prenegotiated. The idea behind this contract is that the signee must adhere to the conditions stipulated by the composer. Communication in this model is linear as opposed to interactional. Similar to Mantan and Sleep 'n Eat's contract, the rhetorical conditions are similar in that the two characters both wanted to assimilate at all costs. Moreover, Dunwitty's understanding of the contract and Delacroix's desire to be accepted as white exploit Delacroix's psychological dilemma. Delacroix has to choose between his blackness and his whiteness. In the subsequent scene, Delacroix officially signs the contract; this act is revealed through the transpiring dialogue.

Delacroix: Dunwitty wants a Coon show. And that's what I'm going to give him. It's going to be so racist, so negative, he won't have the balls to put it on the air. Hence I'll prove my point.
Sloan: Sounds risky to me.
Delacroix: You getting cold feet?
Sloan: I'm in till the end.
Delacroix: Good. I'm going to need your support.
Sloan: Can't you just quit? Walk away?
Delacroix: And lose out on my money? The only way I get paid is if I get fired. And that's what I intend to do.

The supporting cast of information does several things. First, it exemplifies the necessary conditions in which a Ready-to-sign cultural contract materializes. Second, it examines the psychological process of the contractual negotiation process and how social exigencies affect one's autonomy. Finally, the caption foreshadows Delacroix's capitulation and sacrifice that would serve as a means of agency. Delacroix's willingness to cooperate with Dunwitty means that Delacroix would have influential decision-making ability over the racially charged television show; more important, he would gain approval from his white counterparts. This is to say that the tables are reversed. Delacroix would be the composer of the contract instead of Dunwitty. Jackson (2002) expressed the malleable nature of the contract insofar that it is not fixed and stable. Contracts can evolve, transform, and even be breached. Delacroix's psychological disposition is transformed; he thought he was doing the composing instead of the signing. Dunwitty suggested that Delacroix hire a team of writers to help him with the project. As Delacroix sits at the head of a conference table with Sloan and several team members, he silently states to himself: The mission was accomplished. All of these people left the room thinking they would have real input. I was writing this pilot alone.

Delacroix is not privy to the reality of the situation. His involvement with the writers is intentional, by Dunwitty, to ease his perturbed feelings. Dunwitty's intentions are to make the most racist controversial show. Knowing that it will not be met with protest, he does not inform Delacroix or Sloan; he just tells Delacroix the more racist, the better. The rhetorical dilemma is a product of semantic noise. Delacroix feels that he turned the tables on Dunwitty (instead of signing the contract, he is now the composer). Understanding the nature of the rhetorical situation, Dunwitty provides Delacroix with artificial power (the less arduous way is to give Delacroix the impression that he is in control, while all along making revisions to his work). Delacroix realizes the ploy. Delacroix charges in as Dunwitty and Jukka go over the same "pink" revisions.

Delacroix: *I will not be held responsible for these revisions. These changes are not the way I want to go. This in an outrage. This is a sham. A violation!*
Dunwitty: Calm down, please.
Jukka: In Finland, when we get upset—
Delacroix: I don't give a good goddamn about Finland, Norway, Sweden, or wherever ya blond ass came from.
Dunwitty: *We just punched it up a bit. Made it funnier.*
Delacroix: Funnier, to who and at who's expense? Dunwitty, when Negroes start to run amok, the boycotts, when the demonstrations commence, I'm giving them your home address. Let's see how you like it when they picket your lawn in Blackwich, Connecticut.
Dunwitty: I seriously doubt that will happen. Didn't I tell you I know your people better than you do?

In a subsequent dialogue with Sloan, Delacroix realizes that Dunwitty has sole control of the Minstrel Millennium Show.

Sloan: What is your problem?
Delacroix: My problem is Mantan, The New Millennium Minstrel Show.
Sloan: Why did you even come up with that shit if you didn't want it made?
Delacroix: It was the principle... I was making a point. I take pride in my work. Plus, I already told you I wasn't gonna walk away from my money.
Sloan: Fuck da money. Why go through all this effort? Why? Are you looking for love from Dunwitty? For respect? Dunwitty and his likes don't give a goddamn about you. So now what are you gonna do?
Delacroix: *Even if money wasn't an issue, Dunwitty will still go ahead without me and that could be more dangerous.*
Sloan: *Like I said, all this for some twisted distorted sense of principle. Dunwitty, he just tolerates your Negroidal ass, he doesn't respect it.*

If Delacroix had not come to the realization that he wasn't the composer of the contract before, he did now. The italicized print clearly illustrates that the contract remained the same, and Delacroix was the signer. According to a statement by Jackson (2002) that was referred to previously, "By understanding what kind of contract(s) you have as an African American...and determining when and why you signed it is possible to deconstruct your relational position" (p. 48). Delacroix's relationship with Dunwitty was based on selfish motives; he yearned for Dunwitty's approval, honor, and admiration. In simpler terms, he wanted to assimilate and negotiate his blackness for a lighter and less noticeable tone. To this end, without a clear understanding of self-concept, an individual's identity falls victim to a confluence of random social exigencies. To recapitulate the main points,

- Pivotal characters (Cheeba, Manray, Delacroix) illustrate the rhetorical dimensions of a Ready-to-Sign cultural contract.
- Analysis I examines the rhetorical exigencies impelling the characters toward a Ready-to-sign cultural contract.
- Analysis I also highlights the importance of essentialism in the development of cultural contracts.

Contract Theory—Analysis II (*X*)

In this section, the researcher will continue his investigation into cultural contracts of negotiation by scrutinizing Malcolm X as the central character in the film *X* (1992). The first contract examined is a Quasi-completed cultural contract; the second contract examined is a Ready-to-sign cultural contract, followed by another a Ready-to-sign cultural contract, and finally a Cocreated cultural contract.

Quasi-Completed Cultural Contract

> In the film *X*, Malcolm X's identity and negotiation process can best be described as fluid and transient. To understand characteristics of black identity to their fullest capacity, one must approach identity as a set of ideological jigsaw puzzles of expression—whether it is music, literature, sports, history, and so forth. The "matrices of identity are political, for they involve interests, desire, antagonisms, etc. in constant interplay with broad social structures. (Lubiano, 1998, p. 98)

There is no one salient feature available to articulate black identity. With this in mind, the researcher feels that the appropriate manner in which to undertake this study and investigate Malcolm's identity and negotiation process, as presented by Lee (2000), is as a series of evolutions and transformations. There are four phases of Malcolm's life that will be explored: his ongoings with Sophia (Quasi-completed cultural contract), his ongoings with West Indian Archie (Ready-to-sign cultural contract), his relationship with Elijah Muhammad (Ready-to-sign cultural contract) and his relationship with the Nation of Islam and his post-Mecca disposition (Cocreated cultural contract).

In the film *X*, Lee (2000) depicts Malcolm as distressed with issues of identity. Issues of identity and negotiation plagued Malcolm from infancy. The fact that his mom was of a lighter hue and his father of a darker hue set the stage for how Malcolm would relate to others and eventually come to understand himself as a black man.

Malcolm: My mother was fair skinned because her mother was raped by a white man. One of the reasons she married my father was because he was so black. She hated her complexion and wanted her children to have some color. I think this had a profound effect on me today and most Negroes today.

If the argument above explicates a necessary condition for Malcolm's identity crisis, then it is plausible to entertain Malcolm's willingness to both assimilate and rebuff mainstream culture. Prior to Malcolm's years in Mecca, his life can be understood as one wrestling match after another with no clear adversary. It wasn't that Malcolm wasn't able to defeat his opponent; Malcolm was unable to identify the opponent. His inability to identify himself as the adversary led him to exhaust various contracts. This paradox affected Malcolm's social interactions; his thoughts, language, and actions were all contaminated by his crisis. Hall and du Gay (1996) argued that paradoxical worldviews serve as models of real perceptions that are never entirely clear.

Malcolm's first impacting and contractual relationship was with a white female named Sophia. This relationship revealed a candid snapshot of Malcolm's identity crisis. Moreover, it served as a stepping-stone to more complex and involved contracts. Jackson (1999) reported that "there is a constant sense of anxiety endured by African Americans having constantly to constrict their behaviors, lifestyles, and language usage in order to function successfully within specific cultural contexts" (pp. 1–2). Within this line of reasoning, Malcolm's perturbed feelings about his relationship with Sophia become clearer.

Malcolm: What's your story? You one of those white chicks can't get enough colored stud. Kiss my foot. (Sophia complies.) Feed me. (Sophia complies.)
Malcolm: *That's your story, girl. So when you gonna holler rape?*
Sophia: *Me?*
Malcolm: *Yes, you. You would if the time came.* I wish your mother and father could see you now, and that ofay your gonna marry.
Sophia: I sure wish Laura could see us.

Clearly, the contract evident in this relationship is that of a Quasi-completed cultural contract. Jackson (2002) proposed that "people with quasi-completed cultural contracts are not ready to fully value the other's cultural worldview because of the effect they think that it might have on maintaining their worldview" (p. 48). Without going into a historical analysis, Malcolm and Sophia's relationship was prohibited because interracial relationships were not considered appropriate. To this end, segregation and racial tension were at a pinnacle with severe consequences. Sophia and Malcolm had a dubious relationship that wasn't clear, reasons for their relationship were still questionable, and the rewards versus risks didn't quite seem profitable for both parties. Despite the ominous reality and the potential risk evident in their relationship, Malcolm and Sophia still thought a disciplined relationship was mutually satisfying. Whatever the motivations were, they functioned as a bonding element and catalyst for the Quasi-completed cultural contract.

Jackson (2002) identified a necessary, but not a sufficient, condition about a Quasi-completed contract: "With quasi-completed contracts, there is recognition that there is something fundamentally wrong with assimilation, and something equally wrong with polarity" (p. 49). Throughout their relationship, both Malcolm and Sophia had one foot in the door while the other one was out. Their relationship was always marked by both constant arrival and departure because of their race.

What is not clear about the relationship and the contract are the two exigencies making the relationship both possible and elusively enticing: intrapersonal and social. Arguably, Malcolm wanted Sophia just as much as Sophia wanted Malcolm. Culturally and socially, there were no sustaining benefits in establishing an interracial relationship; after all, the racial climate at the time didn't tolerate such behavior. At best, blacks would be sentenced to jail on several life counts; at worst, they would be lawfully or unlawfully murdered. Therefore, the intrapersonal exigencies outfactored any social exigencies. Social exigencies by themselves were not enough for a mutually beneficial relationship or contract to be signed. In this situation, social exigencies may serve as a motive to satisfy a sexual fantasy, a curiosity, or something similar. But if scholars consider the components and the philosophy composing the Quasi-completed cultural contract, then the reasons for the contract become less social and more intrapersonal. Intrapersonally, the contract becomes more malleable, more symbolic, less stagnant, and noncommittal. Moreover, the two participants can increase or decrease their level of assimilation to the contract and each other depending on their level of commitment. This aspect makes intrapersonal exigencies more palatable and less risky. Jackson (2002) submitted that this type of contract precludes that "in order for the relationship to work we both have to negotiate part of our identities, belief systems, expectations, and comfort zones" (p. 49).

Within the framework of Jackson's (2002) theory, Malcolm wanted to remain black, yet desired to have privileges that came with being white (e.g., flimsy hair, white women, respect). There were extenuating motivations for assimilating: most noticeably, Malcolm wanted to increase his stock as a black man. This investigation into the Quasi-completed cultural contract has done several things. Incisively,

- It has provided an argument for Malcolm's turbulent life, explaining sufficient conditions for a Quasi-completed cultural contract.
- It has examined Malcolm's Quasi-completed cultural contract with Sophia.
- It has examined the dubious and nebulous nature of a Quasi-completed cultural contract with focus on intrapersonal exigencies.

Ready-to-Sign Cultural Contract (A)

The next notable phase of Malcolm's life involved his dealings with West Indian Archie. After Malcolm left Boston, his travels took him to Harlem where he worked as a waiter. The pay wasn't very good but it kept him off the street. Still, Malcolm wanted more and his insatiable desires led him to West Indian Archie. West Indian Archie was a hustler. By most people's opinion, Archie was a good person to know in the hustling world. The following dialogue speaks to this point.

Malcolm: So I hear tell you're a good man to know.
Archie: When you hear that?
Malcolm: Boston, where I am from.
Archie: Kiss my neck, I've never even been to Boston.
Malcolm: Like the man said, a man's rep travel.
Archie: Did you just con me?
Malcolm: Yes, sir.
Archie: Why?
Malcolm: *Because I want in. It don't take a lot to know you're already there.*
Archie: *I like you a lot. I like your style. You might just do, Mr. Red.*

Clearly, the contract signed was Ready-to-sign. Designated and marked by a willingness to do whatever it takes to be a part of Archie's tribe, Malcolm's contract was defined according to specific stipulations and rules set by Archie. These stipulations and rules were all part of the assimilation process. The dynamics of this linear relationship exploit several gluing components of this contract (symbolic-linguistic and symbolic-material). All contracts imply that two or more interactants have disparate understandings of the world but feel that an alliance may be meaningful (Jackson, 2002). Each person's motive for sustaining the relationship is partly intrapersonal (i.e., social exchange theory). Aside from the material exchanges bonding the contract were symbolic exchanges. Malcolm's motivation for pursuing the relationship was purely symbolic-material, whereas Archie's motivation was symbolic-linguistic.

Symbolic-Linguistic. Noted in the previous dialogue, both Malcolm and Archie carried the conviction that a man's reputation and name carried significance (Archie moreso than Malcolm). The significance between a name and what it identifies invokes a precise and exact reality brought to life through language. In this context, language is a direct conduit to knowledge as it gives syntax and meaning to a disordered universe. The metaphysical relationship is unequivocally the most significant. The following dialogue illustrates the significant relationship between language and reality.

Malcolm: I'm thinking about my money... six big ones you owe me, right?
Archie: What?
Malcolm: 821. It hit didn't it?
Archie: You didn't have 821.
Malcolm: I threw the slate at you, told you to combinate me.
Archie: You never had it.
Malcolm: I tell you, I did. Sophia was there.
Sophia: Archie, you remember don't you?
Archie: Wait, what do you expect her to say?
Sam: Don't do this.
Malcolm: All right, skip it, but you slippin'.
(Archie gives him the money.)
Sam: *His rep is on the line. So is yours. And Red, if you're lying you're a dead man.*
Malcolm: *You go and tell him that.*

For African Americans, names have a sacred ontological connection with an individual's identity and being. Asante (1998) posited, "Africanity broadcasts identity and being" (p. 19). The fundamental essence of Africanity is "nommo," denoting the psychological and mental aspect of the African (Asante, 2002). If reality is interpretive, language is symbolic and a necessary component to that act. (The researcher is aware that former Malcolm Little and Detroit Red, now Malcolm X, are significant names in terms of what they symbolically represent. However, in Lee's [1992] interpretation of Malcolm X's life, these transitions in Malcolm's life were excluded.) The name "West Indian Archie" is innocuous; it is simply a composite of symbols.

However, the symbolic undertones suggest something quite different. West Indian Archie, a street name, signifies an individual who is malicious, dirty, street savvy, wise, and dastardly. Those who interact with West Indian Archie come to understand him through the signified undertones. Reciprocally, that's who West Indian Archie came to see himself. Language provides people with mental templates that guide their interpretations and notions (Wright & Hailu, 1989).

> Through words we can alter reality; we can bring into being and remove from being; we can shape and change the very structure and essence of what is real. The art of speech becomes the primary mode of moving reality. (McPhail, 1996b, p. 38)

In brief, Archie's motive for creating a contract (Ready-to-sign) was purely symbolic-linguistic. The preceding arguments submitted suggest that Archie wanted to augment the symbolic value and function of his name or as described in the dialogue, his "rep."

Symbolic-Material. Malcolm's motivation for establishing an alliance with Archie was symbolic material. Malcolm wanted wealth and to acquire many of the material signs of prosperity. In addition to wealth, Malcolm gained a sum of street knowledge that would allow him to flourish as a criminal. Noted earlier in the description of Harlem and the psychological depiction of the Negro, some blacks envied white culture and its luxuries (e.g., money, social status, clothes). These were all material acquisitions that Malcolm aspired to have. The following dialogue speaks to this idea.

Malcolm: Because I want in. It don't take a lot to know you're already there.
Archie: I like you a lot. I like your style. You might just do, Mr. Red [Malcolm].

Malcolm was impressed by Archie's wealth and material goods. In other words, Archie represented a direct conduit to success. Whereas Archie's identity was ontologically represented in the symbolic value of his name, Malcolm's identity functioned on material acquisitions.

The notion here is that of a capitalist conceptualization of self. In other words, the self is a set of ideas, which are actualized in their symbolic value that a given culture places on them. People recognize themselves in their commodities; they define themselves with the acquisition of goods and products. Within this paradigm of thinking, the motivation for signing the contract was inextricably linked to capitalism and consumption (symbolic-material). The self then is signified by what it consumes. In effect, goods and resources provide a more precise and tangible concept of identity. As such, the Ready-to-sign cultural contract with Archie represented such a possibility for Malcolm.

The examination of the Ready-to-sign cultural contract brought to surface various ideas:

- Two important components of the Ready-to-Sign contract bring it into fruition: symbolic-linguistic and symbolic-material.
- The impetus for Malcolm signing the contract was to assimilate to a lifestyle otherwise unavailable to him.
- Serving as a template to guide Malcolm's rhetorical vision was the essentialist and seductive notion of the accomplished black, draped and enveloped in all types of flamboyant expression.

Ready-to-Sign Cultural Contract (B)

Malcolm's exodus from New York led him to the pains of the penitentiary and into the harbors of The Most Honorable Elijah Muhammad. The contract designated to the rhetorical context is Ready-to-sign. Malcolm's contract with Elijah Muhammad differed from the one he signed with Archie. Arguably, Malcolm's relationship with Archie was based on ignorance and unawareness of the contract he signed. True, the contract was based on assimilation and total capitulation; however, the rhetorical exigencies were vastly different.

A significant prerequisite to exploring Malcolm's contract is to understand the rhetorical conditions in which the contract was developed. En route to submission or the official signing of the contract, Brother Bains played an instrumental role. By way of mentorship and tutelage, Malcolm willfully submitted, not only to Allah but also to The Most Honorable One, Elijah Muhammad. Equally important, Malcolm had a clearer understanding of his identity than he did in the past, so the contract he signed could be looked over scrupulously.

Before the researcher provides arguments in defense of the contract, he will present two critical rhetorical dialogues that lead to the development of the contract. These developments are just as important as the contract itself, providing the ideological borders, structures, and rules. The dialogues follow Jackson's understanding of identity formation and assimilation

Identity Formation

Bains: If you take one step towards Allah, he'll take two steps towards you. We were a race of kings when the white man crawled on all fours in Europe. Do they know who they are? Do you know where you came from? What is your name?

Malcolm: Malcolm Little.

Bains: That's the name of the slave master that owned your family. You don't even know who you are. You're nothing less than nothing. Who are you?
Malcolm: Look, I'm not shit.

This passage exposes a plausible rationale for Malcolm's submission to the Nation of Islam and Allah. It also illustrates the fluid nature of cultural contracts. Finally, it captures Bains' rhetorical prowess.

Prior to this act, Malcolm exhausted both contracts (Quasi-completed and Ready-to-sign) with Sophia and Archie. To be candid, they just didn't work. In several sections of the research thus far, the unceasing theme is identity crisis. Second, the rhetorical episodes leading to Malcolm's current contract illustrate this crisis and the liquid-like nature of identity and its negotiation. From Sophia to Archie, to Elijah Muhammad, Malcolm exhausted several contracts.

Jackson (2002) noted, "[N]aturally, the nature of these contracts shifts as we mature, discover new approaches, and/or find identity shifting so exhausting that we select one contract as a means of stabilizing our lives" (p. 48). The simile of identity as fluid/paradox contextualizes identity as an evanescent faucet, furiously dispensing water or selves. More important, scholars began to see the self as a series of multiple and transitory narratives couched in social interactions. Hall and du Gay (1996) suggested that identity formation is a matter of opposites and paradoxes, at times coming into conflict with one another. Finally, the rhetorical strength of Bains leads Malcolm to a forlorn condition, stripping Malcolm of his essence and leaving him in a state of quietism. In this state of quietism, Malcolm catches sight of the negative, a universe in which everything is possible but nothing is given. At this moment, Malcolm can decide to accept this universe and draw from it or remain in a state of quietism. In response to Bains' question, "Who are you?" Malcolm replies, "Look, I'm shit."

The depth of humiliation made Malcolm receptive to the discourse of Islam, which brought him much closer to signing another contract. Bensen (1974) noted that a meaningful rhetorical act happens when knowledge and understanding come together. Bensen (1974) located a meaningful rhetorical act in the idea of the praxis. Malcolm's receptivity to Islam is indicative in Bensen's (1974) notion of a rhetorical act. In the ensuing scene and dialogue, Bains brings Malcolm one step closer to Islam. Weighing words carefully, the dialogue explicitly is a list of do's and don'ts, which is non-negotiable. Moreover, conjoining the dialogues purposefully does three things: first, it discusses and describes the true nature of Islam; second, it addresses Islam as a property of complete assimilation; third, it articulates Malcolm's total capitulation to Islam.

Assimilation

Malcolm: I will not touch the white man's poison, his drugs, his liquor, his swine, his women.
Bains: A Muslim must be strikingly upright, an outstanding example so that those in darkness can see power of the light.
Malcolm: I will not commit adultery or fornication. I will not lie, cheat, or steal.
Bains: But the key to Islam is submission. That is why five times daily, we turn to Mecca and pray to bend our knees in submission.
Malcolm: I can't do that Brother Bains.
Bains: The lost found must bend the knees to admit their guilt. To implore Allah's forgiveness is the hardest thing on earth, the hardest and the greatest.
Malcolm: I don't know what I would say to Allah.
Bains: Have you ever been on your knees?
Malcolm: Yes, when I was... picking a lock to rob someone.
Bains: Tell Allah that.
Malcolm: You can grovel and crawl for sin, but not to save your soul.
Bains: Pick the lock, pick it.
Malcolm: I want to. God knows I want to.

Later that night, while Malcolm slept, Elijah Muhammad appeared to Malcolm in a dream. As soon as the vision vanished, he fell on his knees submitting to Allah. Practiced and understood by both black Muslims and Arabic Muslims alike, Islam semantically means to submit. An outward sign, confirming one's compliance, is willfully praying on one's knees, which was something that Malcolm was not ready to do. Bains suggests that this is the ultimate act of surrendering that is tantamount to assimilation.

Assimilation involves more than just a public and private announcement of one's newly found allegiance; it is much more complex. The preceding dialogue points to several interesting components of assimilation. The researcher identifies these as components of Africology (Asante, 1998). The postures of Africology make assimilation possible because they aim to unify and create a sense of being. "There are three fundamental existential postures that one can take with respect to the human condition: feeling, knowing, and acting. Africology recognizes these three stances as being interrelated, not separate" (Asante, 1998, p. 20). These three existential principles are fully engaged within any rhetorical conversion, specifically Islam. Application of the principles impels agency toward a meaningful rhetorical act. Bensen (1974) stated, "Malcolm's existential credentials are strong. He often speaks as if action constitutes the man, and he was a man of action" (p. 6). Begetting any "act," whether it be political or religious, thinking and knowing is the impetus.

Soon after the dialogue between Bains and Malcolm, Malcolm returns to his cell. Malcolm then has a religious vision of Elijah Muhammad who appears amid blinding light. Malcolm then falls on his knees and submits to Allah and Elijah Muhammad. After Malcolm's conversion, he writes relentlessly to his old friends about his newfound faith. He even writes a letter to Bains, conveying that he hasn't written Mr. Muhammad because he hasn't proven himself. The letter reads, "Dear Bros, thanks for your concern, all praises due to Allah for the Honorable Elijah Muhammad. I have dedicated my life to telling the white devil the truth to his face" (Lee, 1992).

The preceding paragraphs bring about the existential and rhetorical postures of Africology to full circle. Indisputably, the paragraphs illustrate the end result of a rhetorical act, which is agency or emancipation (Malcolm's conversion), and the impetus for the act: feeling, thinking, and knowing. As such, these conditions offer immutable evidence of a Ready-to-sign cultural contract.

If the conditions offered suggest the possibility of a Ready-to-sign cultural contract, it is necessary to support the premise. The researcher will direct his attention to rhetorical acts, words, and phrases that reflect the nature of the Ready-to-sign cultural contract. Next, the researcher will illustrate Malcolm's undying commitment to the contract.

Most noticeable are the recurring phraseologies and word choices Malcolm uses before speaking. Prior to speaking, Malcolm prefaces his words with "all praises are due to Allah and his prophet Elijah Muhammad" or "Elijah Muhammad teaches us." Malcolm articulates himself very clearly as the messenger of Elijah Muhammad, holding Mr. Muhammad in the highest esteem. Malcolm refers to Mr. Muhammad as the "Greatest Greatness" and an infallible individual (Lee, 1992). Malcolm's first official speech under the title of National Minister takes place in Harlem. In the opening lines of his speech, he clearly delineates himself from Elijah Muhammad: "I must emphasize at the start that Elijah Muhammad is not a politician. So I'm not here this afternoon as a Republican nor as a Democrat" (Lee, 1992).

In a subsequent scene, Malcolm is preaching in a newly opened Mosque. His speech begins: "I want you to understand one thing. Everything I teach you, everything I have said to you…has been taught to me by this dear man. The divine man. All praises due to Allah for the honorable Elijah Muhammad" (Lee, 1992).

Malcolm also lectured on comparative ideology (nonviolence versus self-defense). Part of his speech follows: "Elijah Muhammad is trying to teach you and I that...the white man and any other man on this earth has the God given right, the human right, and the civil right...to protect himself" (Lee, 1992).

In a panel interview format, Malcolm was asked what the X in his name signifies? He stated, "Elijah Muhammad teaches us that once we come into the knowledge of ourselves, of Islam, the knowledge of ourselves, we replace our slave name with an X...X in mathematics meaning the unknown" (Lee, 1992).

At Harvard University, Malcolm spoke about his criminal days, his involvement with illegal activities, and other illegitimate ongoings that led to his newfound revelation, avowing that, had it not been for Elijah Muhammad, he would either be in prison or dead.

In the subsequent scene, Malcolm is preaching at a Mosque about black politics and Black Nationalism. According to Lee (1992) Malcolm stated, "Mr. Muhammad said these things were gonna come to past, and now they're coming to past. I'm here to tell you about Elijah Muhammad's greatest greatness. His greatest greatness is that he has the only solution for peace in this country. The Honorable Elijah Muhammad's solution is the only solution for you and I. It's the only solution for the white man: complete separation from the black race and the white race."

The preceding excerpts are examples of the number of times Malcolm invokes Elijah Muhammad's name, clearly delineating himself as the messenger of "good news," not the vessel. Although Malcolm has assumed the role of the messenger, he is still the more visible one, attracting controversy, misdirected comments, and a misplaced *ethos*.

The next set of excerpts captures a critical part of his contract, which is total assimilation. The following dialogue offers substantial proof of Malcolm's assimilation, total submission, and capitulation to Islam and Elijah Muhammad. Malcolm's dedication was so sincere that he was called Elijah Muhammad's puppet.

Before Malcolm lectures at Harvard University, a white girl approaches Malcolm. She asks what she and other whites can do to help him and his cause.

White girl: Excuse me, Mr. X. I've read some of your speeches and I honestly believe that a lot of what you have to say is the truth. I'm a good person in spite of what my ancestors did. And I just wanted to ask you: What can a white person like me, who isn't prejudiced...what can I do to help your cause?
Malcolm: Nothing.

Malcolm's commitment to Mr. Muhammad and Islam should not be a question at this point. A central focus of the Nation of Islam is separatism. To remedy the problem of race, blacks must assume cultural, political, social, and religious autonomy in their lives, never to intermingle with whites; this was Mr. Muhammad's solution. Prior to Malcolm's conversion, Bains asked Malcolm if he had ever known any good white person. Malcolm replied, "No." In fact, Malcolm, like those involved with the Nation of Islam, referred to whites as "devils." So when the white girl asked Malcolm if she could help him with his cause, his most honest and direct answer was "No."

The next rhetorical context exhibits Malcolm's commitment to the Nation of Islam and Elijah Muhammad. Unlike the previous dialogue, which illustrates an external assimilation principle (not to intermingle with whites), the next two rhetorical acts touch on the intangible assimilation principles that aren't empirical. They speak of Malcolm's personal convictions to the organization and Mr. Muhammad that testify to an intersubjective type of assimilation. In the next dialogue, a black man stops Malcolm.

Black Man: Yes, yes, hold on, hold on.
Malcolm: Yes, sir, it's all right my brother. How are you?
Black Man: Can I ask you something...anything? Are you Elijah's pimp?
Malcolm: What are you saying brother?
Black Man: His greatest greatness.
Malcolm: Just say what you're saying.
Black Man: If you don't know, man, I feel the sorriest for you.

In another scene, Betty, his wife, discusses a litigation charge brought against Mr. Muhammad, which Malcolm suggests is founded on a bunch of visceral lies.

Malcolm: You think I'm not aware of their accusations. Brother Bains and I discussed it today.
Betty: Bains? Is he your friend?
Malcolm: What is the matter with you?
Betty: Nothing. What's the matter with you? Wake up. Are you so committed that you blinded yourself. You're so dedicated, you can't face the truth? Open your eyes. Open your eyes. You can face death 24 hours a day, but the possibility of betrayal never entered your head.

Both dialogues exude only a small indication of what Malcolm felt for Elijah Muhammad, Islam, and those who made it possible for his conversion. In the film *X* (1992), Malcolm states, "If any wrong was charged to Mr. Muhammad, I would assume the blame, even if it costs me my life, I would go to the electric chair."

Malcolm proclaims in a monologue the following sentiment:

Malcolm: This sweet gentleman, at whose feet I kneeled, gave me the truth from his own mouth. I adored him in the sense of the Latin word adorance, which means to worship and to fear.... I pledge myself to him even if it costs me my life.

After the Nation of Islam has broken Malcolm's faith, Malcolm states, "My faith had been shattered in a way I can never fully describe. Every second of my 12 years with Mr. Muhammad I'd been ready to die for him...I can come to [grips] with death, but not betrayal...not of the loyalty I gave to the Nation of Islam and Mr. Muhammad."

To recapitulate the major points in this section,
- Different rhetorical exigencies foster the Ready-to-sign cultural contract, impelling Malcolm to shift toward another contract.
- The complexity of assimilation (Africology) led Malcolm to the most meaningful rhetorical act—Islam.

Cocreated Cultural Contract

The next section illustrates how Malcolm's newfound epiphany affected his identity. Chronicling the research thus far, Malcolm went from a Quasi-completed cultural contract to two Ready-to-sign cultural contracts, and finally to a Cocreated cultural contract. The following passage illustrates the working of a Cocreated cultural contract:

Malcolm: Internal difference has forced me out of the Nation of Islam. In the past, I have thought and spoke the words of Elijah Muhammad. Everything I said I started with "The honorable Elijah Muhammad teaches us" thus-and-so. That day is over. From now on I speak my own words, and think my own thoughts. Now that I have more independence of action I will use a more flexible approach in working with others to solve this problem.... We must work together to find a common solution to a common problem.

Jackson (2002) noted, "Cocreated cultural contracts are fully negotiable, with the only limits being personal preferences or requirements. This is often perceived as the optimal means of relational coordination across cultures, since the relationship is fully negotiable and open to differences" (p. 49). Moreover, a Cocreated cultural contract recognizes that any contract and communicative interaction has its limitations, maintaining that a synergetic approach toward communicative interactions would prove beneficial. Jackson's (2002) concept is exemplified through Malcolm's letter to his wife, Betty.

Malcolm: Now you may be shocked by these words, but I've eaten from the same plate, drunk from the same glass, and prayed to the same God with Muslims whose eyes were blue, whose hair was blond, and whose skin was the whitest of the white. And we were all brothers...truly people, colors and races believing in one God, in one humanity. In the past, I've made sweeping indictments of all white people. And these generalizations have caused injuries to some whites who didn't deserve them.

Malcolm's transformative rhetoric is best understood as racially and philosophically inclusive, encouraging political leaders, religious leaders, blacks, and whites to form a unilateral alliance; an alliance would allow all groups to transform and morph their identities to think of themselves as "humans" involved in one human struggle (Terrill, 2000). McPhail (1996b) indicated that Malcolm's transformation reflects that of Peitho: "Peitho, the ancient art of rhetoric, empowers precisely because it offers the possibility of change, and the possibility to negotiate the contexts and constraints of communication between persons of reality, and of power" (p. 38). Peitho describes Malcolm's ability to transcend his partisan feelings about race and political and social issues, and make favorable strides to rectify those matters through a rhetoric of cooperativeness and transcendence. If the letter is examined carefully, the logic permeating the discourse is that of a comparative rhetoric. Malcolm carefully makes use of the international and the national race relation scene to identify him and other blacks within the American racial and political struggle. By using a comparative front, he reconceptualizes the race issue, not as a black or white problem but as a human issue.

> Since I learned the truth in Mecca, my dearest friends have come to include all kinds—some Christians, Jews, Buddhists, Hindus, agnostics and even atheists! I have friends who are called capitalists, socialists, communists! Some of my friends are moderates, conservatives, extremists—some are even Uncle Toms! My friends today are black, yellow, and white! (Bensen, 1974, p. 5)

> [Impaling Malcolm's rhetoric] was a well-groomed ethos, that which led his audience away from a narrow focus of American racism and invited them to share with him a larger but perhaps more detached and [paradoxical] context within which to frame the problem. (Bensen, 1974, p. 72)

And it is precisely this humanist ethos that attracts and alienates both whites and blacks alike.

Reporter: Malcolm, you sensed a feeling of Brotherhood.
Malcolm: Yes, when I was in Mecca, making the pilgrimage, the

brotherhood that existed there among all people, all races, all levels of people, who had accepted the religion of Islam. Today, my friends are black, red, yellow, brown, and white.

Reporter: Will you work now with leaders of other civil rights or organizations?

Malcolm: Yes, we're prepared to work with any group leaders or organizations as long as they're genuinely interested in results...positive results.

Terrill (2000) noted, Malcolm encouraged the members of his audience [both white and black] to abandon their limited perspective of identity, race, and politics. Malcolm invited them to refashion their identities and thus become a "people," rather than that which the dominant culture has told them they must be. There will always be interminable cultural and religious differences between humans. Nevertheless, having differences doesn't suggest that cultures can't work together. McPhail (1996b) noted, Peitho "enables us to move beyond argumentative [and cultural] essentialism to some common ground of understanding" (p. 35).

Malcolm's discourse gives people reason to believe that a rhetoric of integration and cooperation is possible. This doesn't suggest that Malcolm has alienated Black Nationalism, a key philosophical and economical strategy within his rhetoric of liberation (Painter, 1993; Reid, 1993). Malcolm clearly acknowledges that there cannot be any white/black solidarity without black solidarity; the same would stand true for whites, or for any other group.

In *X* (1992), Malcolm's bipartisan politics creates a rhetorical and cultural shock, which ultimately alienates him. This is quite understandable. Malcolm was rejected in his native homeland and from several nations abroad. From his hell-like and unforgiving rhetoric toward whites, to his benevolence and warm embracing of whites, his identities as black, Muslim, and political leader are all subject to scrutiny. Moreover, Malcolm's inconsistent rhetoric imploded as his revolutionary requests to various audiences proved to be daunting and incredulous. Malcolm made concerted efforts to reconcile differences and forge alliances with all those who believed in his new cause, those who he labeled an Uncle Tom, Devil, or other such debasing words. In short, he burned too many bridges that could not be repaired.

> For some, he had left the "dreaded" and misunderstood Nation of Islam with its fire and brimstone religious nationalism... For others he was now seemingly making a concerted effort to be all things to all people and was willing to practice brotherhood with any sincere White persons. (Leader, 1993, p. 152)

Although cultural harmony might have been the goal, Malcolm lost sight of the stark and grave reality of the disease that plagued him and all humans—racism and irreconcilable ideological differences. The very choleric rhetoric that afforded Malcolm an unquestionable ethos was the same rhetoric that rendered him questionable.

> Malcolm failed to realize that it is impossible for true brotherhood to exist between the exploiter and the exploited, the oppressor and the oppressed, or the Dominant Group and the Submissive Group...because each group has a different belief system; some in direct conflict with each other. Second, for our purposes, when these factions are reduced to combinations making up various factions of the Dominant Group and the Submissive Group, the Dominant Group will effectuate policies designed to maintain its superordinate position. (Leader, 1993, p. 153)

Malcolm's commitment to this new contract created a terrible feeling of estrangement, coupled with a deathly feeling of solipsism and uncertainty toward The Nation of Islam and any organized group. Malcolm had no assurance that other organization's motives were genuine, simply because they overtly share similar philosophies. Lee (1992) highlighted Malcolm's cynicism in a statement that Malcolm makes to Brother Earl: "Have faith in Allah, not in mankind." In the film, Malcolm's cynicism escalates into solipsism when he feels his death encroaching; yet, he still walks into the ballroom for his final speech.

Earl: Malcolm, what's wrong?
Malcolm: It's a time for martyrs now... The way I feel... I shouldn't go out there.

Despite Malcolm's uncertainty about his future, he committed the ultimate act—he confronted the absurd and gave his final speech. Malcolm's comment to Earl was the height and the pinnacle of his rhetorical and contractual ethos. Like the other contracts he exhausted, they had measurable consequences and penalties that changed him altogether; however, the Cocreated cultural contract was different in that it required total assimilation; this was a prerequisite that could only be quantified but never truly be understood qualitatively.

Malcolm was in a state of despair because he could never conceive of the wrongdoings that were inflicted on him. Malcolm sadly realized that verbal communication was no longer available as an effective means of persuasion and harmony. The paradox was that a great man of words fell speechless. Arguably, this is Malcolm's tragedy.

The examination of the Cocreated cultural contract brings to the surface various ideas about

- The transitory shift to a Cocreated cultural contract
- How Malcolm's shift to a Cocreated cultural contract altered his identity
- How the shift affected him internally

The end of the previous three sections consists of grappling with the research questions, which appear in Chapter V.

V
Analysis Questions

(Q1) How do Ready-to sign cultural contracts, Quasi-completed cultural contracts, and Cocreated cultural contracts affect black identity in the films *Bamboozled* (2000) and *X* (1992)?

Within the domain of Du Bois' (1903) theory of "double-consciousness" and Watts' (2002) theory of "hermeneutical ethos," cultural contracts affect black identity in that the contracts allow for one to be self-reflexive. Second, cultural contracts are vehicles to self-agency as both Du Bois (1903) and Watts (2002) underscore in their theories.

Double-Consciousness

The impact of these cultural contracts on black identity allows one to have a keen sense of awareness about his or her various selves and how they are perceived. In this manner, cultural contracts bring to light the various parts of one's identity. Cultural contracts, in this regard, suggest that the social context of a particular communicative situation can make various aspects of an individual's identity more or less accessible to him or her. In the films, most of the characters are struck with a revelation about themselves as a result of their contractual interactions.

Du Bois' (1903) theory of "double-consciousness" provides clarity to this issue as it speaks to the type of self-reflexivity and revelation that the researcher is arguing. Du Bois (1903) noted that "double-consciousness" is a self-realization that one is different because of his or her race and ideology. What transpires from this realization is a veil. Du Bois (1903) noted, "Then it dawned upon me with a certain suddenness that I was different from the others; or like, mayhap, in heart and life and longing, but shut out from their world by a vast veil" (p. 2). (Although one may argue that the veil Du Bois [1903] spoke about is one that has to do with race, one should also realize that Du Bois truly didn't understand the severity of the race issue until he matriculated at Fisk University). Du Bois' (1903) prophetic words suggest that the veil of difference produces a sensitivity—an awareness of one's self that always exists when communicating with those who are different, with respect to race, beliefs, and convictions.

Du Bois (1903) stated, "It is a peculiar sensation, this 'double consciousness,' this sense of always looking at one's self through the eyes of others... One ever feels his twoness—an American, a Negro; two souls, two thoughts" (p. 3). To this end, contracts are more than ways in which blacks may negotiate their identity; contracts are a self-realization that one has to experience this twoness that manifests itself through a veil. For example, in the film *Bamboozled* (2000), Cheeba realizes that no matter how much success he might enjoy, or respect he would acquire from a popular show, it would never be good enough. He would always be looked at as a second-class citizen.

Du Bois (1903) noted that racism constructs "blackness" as a problematic sign and an essential problem. Racist discourse supports the belief that black communities, black artifacts, are the carriers of danger and social problems. Cheeba comes to this realization and decides not to continue with the minstrel performance. This realization is made possible through a "double-consciousness."

Cheeba: I'm not drinking the Kool-Aid.
Mantan: What are you talkin' about?
Cheeba: Jim Jones, y' know. I'm not drinking the Kool-Aid.
Mantan: Meaning?
Cheeba: I'm out.

This short but powerful scene addresses an important aspect of cultural contracts, as it speaks to Du Bois' (1903) statement of "double-consciousness." The central component to Du Bois' (1903) theory is self-revelation about individuals' collective and conflictive identities. No individual belongs to just one socially constructed class. Each individual is unique and has multiple identities. These identities are flexible and malleable and change according to an individual's social interest. The dialogue between Cheeba and Mantan clearly illustrates that Cheeba's interest in the show is no longer compatible with Mantan's. In other words, Cheeba's social interest changed. As a result Cheeba's identity is now in conflict with Mantan's.

To be aware of individuals' many communicative selves is to understand the enormous collective social composition that influences who people are. As such, people must recognize that their identities are disjointed, and frailty can be disconcerting, especially when there is nothing absolute on which to ground identities. When Mantan reacts to Cheeba's decision, he is astonished. To Mantan, Cheeba's identity is firmly grounded in the character Sleep 'n Eat. Cheeba is a distant memory. Outside of the character Sleep 'n Eat, there is no other possible identity for Cheeba. Mantan is never aware of the dynamic, frail, and disjointed nature of identity, until the latter parts of the film. Like Cheeba, Manray comes to a starling revelation. This revelation is captured in the following scene.

Delacroix: Mantan, we got a show to tape.
Mantan: My name is Manray, goddamn it.
Delacroix: You go back to your dressing room, get dressed and blacken up.
Manray: I'm not playin' myself no mo'.
Delacroix: How you sound?
Manray: I won't do it anymore.

The significance of this scene is that Manray decides to perform, but without blackface. Arguably, his reluctance not to blacken up, but to perform, indicates that there is something fundamentally wrong with negotiating his identity in that manner. The thought of blackening up is twisted and sordid and weighs heavy on his heart. This change of mind is the recognition of a "double-consciousness."

Du Bois (1903) noted, "double-consciousness" is the recognition that black identity is multifaceted. And at any given time blacks are in constant turmoil with their cultural identity, their public identity, what their identity communicates to others, and what it means to negotiate these identities. All of these dimensions are critical to understanding black identity and the characters' dilemma in the film.

It is not enough to recognize the conflictive nature of black identity. By understanding black identity, one can negotiate it more effectively and use it to his or her advantage. The realization of black identity as inclusive of a "double-consciousness" is liberating because one has a keener sense of self and identity. In this line of reasoning, "double-consciousness" is a means to agency and freedom (Du Bois, 1903). "Double-consciousness" does not mean that blacks are necessarily damaged, although racial oppression plays a significant role in the way African Americans perceive themselves. Du Bois (1903) recognized that African Americans can forge a healthy, strong self-concept even with the stigma of being devalued by the larger society. "Double-consciousness" reminds people that they are always free to act by their own will. Even though others might perceive them differently, even those from their own race, individuals always have agency. An individual may not be free as to exercise a physical autonomy; there will always be some restrictions, but he or she always has the choice to exercise his or her virtues, which reaffirms an existential freedom. Du Bois (1903) stated that education is the vehicle to freedom. More important, it is a way to weaken the veil, to exercise agency, to make prudent choices, and to build a stronger sense of self and identity. This ability to make prudent choices and build a stronger sense of identity speaks to Watts' (2002) vision of a "hermeneutical ethos" for blacks.

Hermeneutical Ethos

In Du Bois' (1903) *The Souls of Black Folk,* he argued that education could begin to remove the veil. This was a starting point, and because racism exists, education was and still is the key. The term "education" in this context signifies agency, self-empowerment, and understanding. These ideas are best understood as a "hermeneutical ethos." A "hermeneutical ethos" goes one step beyond "double-consciousness." "Double-consciousness" affirms a discernment, awareness, revelation, or a rhetorical vision. A "hermeneutical ethos" is a grassroots effort to make social change or to carry out one's revelation and rhetorical vision. The examples to follow clearly focus on the execution of the characters' revelation and rhetorical vision.

In both of Lee's films, *Bamboozled* (2000) and *X* (1992), the characters, on whom the researcher focuses, were engulfed in various cultural contracts. Some of these characters found the contracts daunting and never experienced liberation and agency; however, those who recognized this empowerment exemplified a "hermeneutical ethos." The following example illustrates what the researcher believes to be the perfect example of Watts' (2002) "hermeneutical ethos." In no fewer than two scenes separating the following dialogue, Lee (1992) depicts Malcolm in a state of despair, then in an unexpected state of optimism.

Malcolm: This sweet gentleman, at whose feet I kneeled, gave me the truth from his own mouth. I adored him in the sense of the Latin word adorance, which means to worship and to fear.... I pledge myself to him even if it costs me my life.

After Malcolm's faith had been broken by the Nation of Islam, Malcolm stated,

My faith had been shattered in a way I can never fully describe. Every second of my 12 years with Mr. Muhammad I'd been ready to die for him.... I can come to [grips] with death, but not betrayal...not of the loyalty I gave to the Nation of Islam and Mr. Muhammad. Internal difference has forced me out of the Nation of Islam. In the past, I have thought and spoke the words of Elijah Muhammad. Everything I said I started with "The honorable Elijah Muhammad teaches us" thus-and-so. That day is over. From now on I speak my own words, and think my own thoughts. Now that I have more independence of action, I will use a more flexible approach in working with others to solve this problem.... We must work together to find a common solution to a common problem.

The researcher finds this scene life affirming. In the first monologue, Malcolm comes to the realization that his contract expires, and there is nothing more that he can do. Instead of succumbing to the ill will that his adversaries give him, he takes control over his own predicament. Watts (2002) noted, "One's competence can be assessed in terms of propriety or prudence.... In this regard both rhetoric and hermeneutical ethos are oriented by one's sense of the proper orchestration, characterization, and articulation of topical material in accordance with one's lived experience" (p. 22). Watts' (2002) comment amplifies how one's identity is affected by a "hermeneutical ethos." Malcolm's decision is reflective of a "hermeneutical ethos" in that his belief and actions are based on the core conviction that the meaning of a doctrine is the same as the practical effects of adopting it. In other words, Malcolm's belief in his new inclusive organization is measured by the organization's ability to achieve its aims. As such, there is a relationship between one's self and the discourse one embodies (Watts, 2002); this relationship is the benchmark of a "hermeneutical ethos." According to X (1992), Malcolm stated, "Now that I have more independence of action, I will use a more flexible approach in working with others to solve this problem.... We must work together to find a common solution to a common problem."

Unlike the Nation of Islam, Malcolm is not seeking an individual solution to a universal problem. Malcolm sees the issue much larger than that. Malcolm realizes that the only solution to the issue of race is one that is inclusive of all races working together. Those who are European, African American, and any other nationality, who are genuinely concerned with results, are invited to help Malcolm. Watts (2002) noted that those seeking agency seek it on the basis of the degree to which it is ethical, inspirational, free, creative, and motivational. In this light, a "hermeneutical ethos" leads to self-clarification and results that are tangible and real. Watts (2002) noted that a "hermeneutical ethos" must, if it is to accomplish its revolutionary aim, deal in clear and focused terms. Malcolm's vision for his new political movement was focused and clear. In short, a "hermeneutical ethos" seeks to produce and provide honest, practical, pragmatic knowledge that is judged by the degree to which it achieves action. Malcolm's new rhetorical approach toward culture and difference was trustworthy and authentic. This approach replaced the dogmatic and rigid hermeneutical ethos. The adoption of this approach transformed the minds of many and provided Malcolm with a new ethos.

Watts (2002) noted that the New Negro evolves from a "hermeneutical ethos." A "hermeneutical ethos" "emerges as a hero from a new era, embodying a trangressive notion of race and culture. Moreover, he is a topical resource of ongoing rhetorical invention and praxis" (Watts, 2002, p. 20). He or she refuses to be defined by the same traditional concepts of identity and humanity; moreover, he or she evolves out of a language that is all his or her own. Evidence of this idea can be found in Malcolm's soliloquy in *X* (1992).

Malcolm: In the past, I have thought and spoke the words of Elijah Muhammad. Everything I said I started with "The honorable Elijah Muhammad teaches us" thus-and-so. That day is over. From now on I speak my own words, and think my own thoughts.

To this end, Watts (2002) suggested that this more competent and assiduous psyche leads toward a new type of "hermeneutical ethos." In addition to the important commentary Malcolm makes about his new political agenda, what emerges from the discourse of Malcolm is an authentic voice. A result of a "hermeneutical ethos" is voice. Voice is a critical component to any ethical transformation (Watts, 2002). Voice is the struggle to figure out how an individual is to present his or her ideas and represent his or her own personal accounts. Voice is the acknowledgement that one does not want to be silenced (Watts, 2002). Malcolm's voice and social and political vision is made possible through the discourse of "hermeneutical ethos."

The following points address the research question: How do Ready-to-sign cultural contracts, Quasi-completed cultural contracts, and Cocreated cultural contracts affect black identity in the films *Bamboozled* (2000) and *X* (1992)?

- Using both Du Bois' (1903) and Watts' (2002) theories, the contracts affect black identity in that they are self-reflexive. The impact of these cultural contracts on black identity allows one to have a keen sense of awareness about his or her various selves and how they are perceived. In this manner, cultural contracts bring to light the various parts of one's identity.
- Second, cultural contracts serve as a means to agency, specifically through the use of a "hermeneutical ethos." A "hermeneutical ethos" is empowering because its epistemological tenets focus on change.

(Q2) What are the consequences for breaching contracts in the films *Bamboozled* (2000) and *X* (1992)?

In order to answer this question, the researcher will first provide a definition of a "broken contract." A breached or broken contract occurs when the signer or signee refuses to continue participating in a communicative act. Jackson (2002) stated that all people break contracts, negotiate new ones, and so forth. "Naturally, the nature of these contracts shifts as we mature, discover new approaches..." (Jackson, 2002, p. 48). Jackson's (2002) statement speaks to the continuous acculturation process, which is a natural part of human interaction and communication. Second, the researcher will address this question within the theoretical parameters of West's (1993) theory of "alienation." Evolving from "alienation" are two types of tragic heroes: The first type of tragic hero is one who decides to battle or take a stand against repressive ideological conventions that pose as normal and customary parts of culture. By transcending a universal cultural ethic, the tragic hero stands for something authentic.

The second type of tragic hero is confused about his or her contract and strives for something authentic and virtuous but dies in that pursuit, falling victim to his or her own uncertainty and predicament. In both types of tragedy resides a point of "alienation."

However, Jackson's (2002) statement doesn't mention what happens in the transitory period after the contract is broken between contracts. West (1993) provided an account of this phenomenon through his notion of "alienation."

Alienation

"Alienation" is similar to "double-consciousness" in that they are both black existential terms, but that is where their similarity ends. "Double-consciousness" lays out the cultural problems confronting the African American, whereas "alienation" describes the psychological absurdity in the problem. "Alienation" is the result of a broken contract; it is humankind in its most psychologically emaciated state, without any gods, ideologies, idols, or fears. In short, alienation is humankind at its freest existence. This existence allows individuals to know their dasein through which individuals become newly acquainted with themselves. West (1993) described "alienation" as "the wandering between worlds, one dead the other powerless to be born" (p. 6). In this state, humankind finds itself somewhere between the two worlds of existence. "Alienation" is marked by absurdity, which gives rise to authenticity or inauthenticity. West (1993) stated that a key component to alienation is responsibility and authenticity, which allows one to feel free. In other words, an individual cannot be free unless he or she trusts him- or herself and is honest and acts accordingly to his or her own virtues and subjectivity. When one accepts oneself as an authentic and unique being, West stated (1993), they are acting authentic. On the other hand, "alienation" can give way to anxiety, which can lead to inauthenticity. Inauthenticity is when one does not take responsibility for who he or she is. Inauthenticity is when one acts against his or her own virtue and subjectivity. Often, an inauthentic individual is one who acts according to what others prescribe. In other words, it is a false type of existence. The following examples identify broken contracts and "alienation" as the effect of a breached contract. After citing the four examples of "alienation," the researcher will elaborate more on the concept of "alienation" as it relates to characters.

In the first example, Delacroix is privy to the information that he will not have control over the contents of his show. As a result, he psychologically resigns.

Delacroix: Yes, I know. Jukka, have you ever seen a Negro person before? Ever had a real conversation with a real Negro before?
Jukka: What's a Negro?

Delacroix continues to rant and rave. He looks like he has seen a ghost as he buries his face into his hands. He is aware of his actions and the possible ramifications of such a show but can't figure out how to sabotage the beast he created.

Delacroix: Did you just ask me What's a Negro? This is a fiasco, a disaster.

In the next scene, Sleep 'n Eat talks to Mantan about the situational comedy and decides to resign from the show.

Sleep 'n Eat: I'm not drinking the Kool-Aid.
Mantan: What are you talkin' about?
Sleep 'n Eat: Jim Jones, y' know. I'm not drinking the Kool-Aid.
Mantan: Meaning?
Sleep 'n Eat: I'm out.

In the ensuing scene, Mantan decides to resign as well. Mantan looks at his makeup laid out before him on the counter and stares at himself in the dressing room mirror. Mantan can't stand to blacken up anymore. As the show commences, Mantan walks on stage without his costume and blackface.

Delacroix: Mantan, we got a show to tape.
Mantan: My name is Manray, goddamn it.
Delacroix: You go back to your dressing room, get dressed and blacken up.
Manray: I'm not playin' myself no mo'.
Delacroix: How you sound?
Manray: I won't do it anymore.

Finally, in the film *X* (1992), Malcolm decides to break away from The Nation of Islam and initiate a new political and religious effort. Malcolm states, "Internal difference has forced me out of The Nation of Islam." According to *X* (1992), Malcolm states,

My faith had been shattered in a way I can never fully describe. Every second of my 12 years with Mr. Muhammad, I'd been ready to die for him.... I can come to [grips] with death, but not betrayal...not of the loyalty I gave to the Nation of Islam and Mr. Muhammad.

It is during these brief moments in which one becomes conscious that existence is possible. Because one is no longer a stranger to him- or herself, he or she pays the ultimate price—absolute responsibility, which is tantamount to death. Yet, the irony remains, a person is most free in this state. The examples to follow illustrate this statement.

The following rhetorical act shows the consequence of Mantan's actions. A revolutionary rap group of African Americans disapprove of Mantan's petulant behavior and decide that his behavior is irreconcilable.

Big Black: You is one dead nigger.
Manray: What did I do?
Big Black: What did you do? Brothers, he asks what did he do?
Double Black: If you don't know, there is nuthin' we can do for you.
Big Black: Nigga, you will be executed.

The next dialogue examines Delacroix and the punitive measure bestowed on him.

Sloan: Get up and put that tape in.
(Sloan points the gun at Delacroix's head).
Do what I say.
(Delacroix takes the cassette tape off his desk and puts it in the player.)
Delacroix: I don't think this was in your studies at NYU.
(Delacroix hits the play button. Images. History. Visuals. Sloan has put together a tape of the worst, most racist stereotypical images from cinema and television over the last 100 years. With these images, there is also a laugh track.)
Sloan: Watch, this is what you contributed to. Because of you, Manray is dead. My brother is dead. It's all because of you.
(Delacroix can't watch the monitor.)
Delacroix: I'm sorry. I didn't know anyone would get hurt. I'm sorry, please give me the gun before you hurt yourself. Give me the gun.
(Delacroix reaches for the gun. Boom! Sloan screams. Delacroix is dead.)

In the last example, the consequences for Malcolm's actions (broken contract) are no different from the preceding examples. In this scene, Malcolm is at the theatre about to deliver his speech. Earl states:

Earl: Malcolm, what's wrong?
Malcolm: It's a time for martyrs now... The way I feel... I shouldn't go out there.

Several men murdered Malcolm in 'cold blood' soon after he started his speech.

All four examples show renditions of "alienation." "Alienation" is marked by two types of tragic heroes. The first type of tragic hero is one who decides to battle or take a stand against repressive ideological conventions that pose as normal and customary parts of culture. By transcending a universal cultural ethic, the tragic hero stands for something authentic.

The second type of tragic hero is one who is confused about his or her disposition and strives for something authentic and virtuous but dies in that pursuit, falling victim to his or her own uncertainty and predicament. For example, Delacroix exemplifies the second type of hero. As Delacroix pleads for his life, Sloan decides to shoot him. Delacroix's predicament is such that he never knows his true purpose and function within the television network. He never understands his contract, why he signed it, and the ramifications for signing the contract. There is no possible way for him to break the contract on his own accord; he just has to follow the consequences of the contract. His last words with Sloan articulate this uncertainty.

Delacroix: I'm sorry. I didn't know anyone would get hurt. I'm sorry. Please give me the gun before you hurt yourself. Give me the gun.

Unfortunately, there was nothing that Delacroix could do for penance and nothing for reparations. Although he apologizes, his prayers and requests fall on deaf ears. Delacroix's words never change Sloan's intentions. Delacroix pays the ultimate price: a tragic death.

Manray's condition is similar to that of Delacroix's in that he is uncertain about the constituents of his contract. Toward the end of the film, he breaks the contract by refusing to perform, but the damage has been done. Like Delacroix, he finds himself in the clutches of his own predicament, which leads to his own demise. The following words speak to his fate.

Big Black: Brothers, he asks what did he do?
Double Black: If you don't know, there is nuthin' we can do for you.

The tragedy of Manray's existence is also his predicament: his eagerness to sign his contract without understanding the nature of the contract. This predicament exposed him, making him vulnerable to any persuasive discourse and taking away any agency he had. Manray is a composite of several societal undertakings; this fragmentation led him to a morose state. Manray can be described in two different lights. Manray was an African American living the Eurocentric dream. But in the Mau-Maus perspective he was a Judas, or an "Uncle Tom," whose corrupt wrongdoings contributed to the demise of a race.

When Manray presents himself as the revolutionary instead of an object of ridicule, his efforts vaporize. In other words, there are two models of presentation and representation: the audience's and Manray's. These two models are polarities and in conflict with one another, which contributes to Manray's incredulous ethos and ultimately to his demise. Manray's model of himself is interchangeable; it is fluid and amorphous, whereas the audience's model of representation is more stable and rigid. Within this context, Manray's death is inevitable.

Malcolm's death is best understood as the first type of tragic hero: one who decides to battle or take a stand against repressive ideological conventions that pose as normal and customary parts of culture. By transcending a universal cultural ethic, the tragic hero stands for something authentic, thus fulfilling his or her own prophecy.

The tragedy of Malcolm's existence resides in his inability to critically evaluate his own transcendental ethos. Bensen (1974) stated that Malcolm's downfall was that he failed to recognize real differences in the world, differences of religion, differences of politics, and differences of race. In fact, Lee (1992) showed Malcolm's wife reporting in a letter that Malcolm's bipartisan politics are becoming one. He no longer identifies religious practitioners as Jews, Muslims, Christians, and Buddhists; he sees them as humans serving one God in multiple forms.

To the rest of the world, Malcolm stood for something that was never thought to actually exist. Malcolm's tragedy remains in his attempt to surmount the logical and the rational landscape and culture of his time, expecting others to whole-heartedly embrace this vision. By committing to a pluralistic worldview, Malcolm's discourse transcended what was thought to be common sense in his time. In essence, Malcolm fell in love with his own vision of racial and political harmony. Malcolm's death was a result of his own hypnotic and mystical vision. Stated earlier, Malcolm's conversion led him to a new way of understanding, seeing, thinking, and knowing. This thinking propelled him to his death. But his death is not so straightforward. Malcolm's death is what gives his life meaning; it is a battle against the absurdity of life. It is life. To recapitulate the main points of a broken contract,

- The ramification of a broken contract leads to a state of "alienation," man in an identity crisis. He feels a sense of despair because he has no idols, gods, or philosophies of consolation, just his fears making way for his first sign of existence.

- According to Lee (2001), Delacroix, Cheeba, Manray, and Malcolm experience "alienation" in different ways. Delacroix's dasein evolves throughout the film, finally manifesting itself through the culminating interaction with Dunwitty and Jukka. When Delacroix finds out that he has only been a tool, he enters into a state of protest, followed by quietism.
- Unlike Manray and Delacroix, Cheeba doesn't allow external social forces to corner him into a state of "alienation" (Lee, 2001). Rather, the consequences of "alienation" are the impetus and motivation for Cheeba to break his contract.
- Uncertain about the constituents of his contract, Manray never cares about the fine print (Lee, 2001). "Alienation" does not bring Manray to self-resolution; it only brings him to the realization that he is going to die. Malcolm's experience with "alienation" leads him to an unperturbed state of being—a higher sense of resolve.

"Alienation" is an uncontrolled variable. It functions differently for each character. On one hand, it might bring an individual into a higher state of being. On the other hand, it might challenge an individual's intimate belief systems, causing him or her to re-evaluate his or her ideology. All four characters, quite different in their experiences with "alienation," are transformed into tragic heroes, leading them to different types of death.

VI
Overview

This study brought a new perspective toward the continued investigation of the negotiation of black identity. After the careful examination of Spike Lee's *Bamboozled* (2000) and *X* (1992), even more questions are raised about black identity. In review, the researcher set out to do three things: first, explore complicity and essentialist discourse as they relate to the formation of cultural contracts and black identity; second, examine the characters' entering into the cultural contracts and how the contracts affected the characters' identity; third, examine the characters breaching of the contracts in the films; and last, discuss future implications for this study and his contribution to the study of black identity.

Formation of Cultural Contracts

Cultural contracts are predicated upon human interactions and experiences. Human interactions and experiences are important because humans are constantly interacting with one another. Based on human experience and interaction, humans form opinions about one another. Often, these opinions can be hasty or careful. In either case, human judgment marks the formation of a cultural contract. Cultural contracts are formed through essentialist discourse and the belief in foundationalism (McPhail, 1996b). Essentialist and foundationalism is the belief that all things have an essence. In addition, it is the belief that ideas and people are not dynamic; rather, they are static. Specific evidence of this can be found in the discussion topics concerning Harlem and blacks. For blacks, Harlem signifies more than a geographical location. Harlem, in *Bamboozled* (2002) and *X* (1992), is a bastion of hope and a utopia.

Second, both *Bamboozled* (2000), and *X* (1992) articulate blacks as the same: avaricious, hasty, and inept. Although this is the furthest from the truth, Lee (1992, 2000) communicated these ideas through the characters of Cheeba, Manray, Delacroix, and Malcolm X. The viewers' first introduction to these characters reconfirms the central notions mentioned previously. The irony is that although these characters have flaws, they change. However, the argument can be made that these characters fundamentally are avaricious, hasty, and inept. More specifically, these assumptions are the impetus for communicative interactions, and ultimately are a precursor for the formation of a cultural contract.

In both films *Bamboozled* (2000) and *X* (1992), cultural contracts function as a set of restraints. These restraints affect the characters' communication and behavior. Inevitably, the restraints impinge upon the characters identity. Consider, for example, Delacroix, Manray, Cheeba, and Malcolm X. These characters' identity is influenced by the contract they sign. The complicit nature of the contract provides an essentialist vision of the characters' identity. As such, Lee (1992, 2000) provided the viewer with a limited perspective of the characters and their identities. McPhail (1996b) noted that essentialist discourse seduces people into believing that a thing or an idea has a true essence. Indicative in both films is that black identity is a fluid concept; however, black identities are complex and multiple and grow out of a history of changing responses to economic, political, and cultural forces—almost always to other identities. Black identity, in this sense, is fluid and not fixed. It is relative or relational. In summary, this dissertation reports that essentialist discourse has an effect on black identity. It also argues that cultural contracts affect a person's identity and how they are understood.

Characters and the Contracts

The characters examined in the cultural contracts were Delacroix, Manray, Cheeba, and Malcolm X. The contracts that they were placed into were Ready-to-sign, Quasi-completed, and Cocreated. These contracts were a set of ideological restraints—meaning, the nature of the contract restricted the characters' ethos. For example, a Ready-to-sign contract signified that the character could not act or speak on his own accord. A Ready-to-sign contract means that one is in total compliance with the discourse or person. A Quasi-completed contract means that mutual consent is needed in a communicative act, but there is something fundamentally wrong with the relationship. This relationship is marked by uncertainty about the communicative relationship. Therefore, the participants are continually negotiating, until both parties are comfortable. Finally, a Cocreated contract is a contract in which total trust and certainty is gained. There is nothing fundamentally wrong with assimilation. And, in order for the relationship to work, everyone involved has to participate. In summary, cultural contracts are important because they affect the human relationships, and they set limitations and restraints for communication and interaction.

The effects of the contracts on the characters are the most interesting part of this research. McPhail (1996a) communicated the theory of "negative difference," which suggests that all things have an essence and can be understood in terms of a specific quality. However, once the characters entered the cultural contracts, their identity changed. The notion that black identity is dynamic comes into fruition. An excellent example of this can be found in the film *X* (1992). In *X* (1992), Malcolm enters and exits three contracts: a Ready-to-sign, a Quasi-completed, and a Cocreated contract. As a result of each contract, Malcolm's identity changes.

Just as important as the contract itself is the noticeable shift in character name. There seems to be a relationship between the cultural contract and the shifting of the characters' names. Consider, for example, Malcolm X. Malcolm was called "Red," "Minister," and "X." These names had a profound effect on Malcolm's demeanor and how he interacted with people. Lee (1992) reported that Malcolm was transformed from a criminal into one of the most positive and influential African-American political activists. As reported in this document, Malcolm evolved into a hero.

Another example of the significance of characters' names includes the characters in *Bamboozled* (2000): Delacroix, Cheeba, Manray, Jungle Bunny, Snowflake, Sambo, Aunt Jemima, Rastus, and Nigger Jim. Reported previously, for African Americans, names have a sacred ontological connection with one's identity and being. Asante (1998) posited, "Africanity broadcasts identity and being" (p. 19). The fundamental essence of Africanity is "nommo," denoting the psychological and mental aspect of the African. As this research reports, the embracing of these racist names has tremendous effects on the overall psyche of the character.

Breaching of Cultural Contracts

The principle question that addresses black identity and the cultural contract is: What are the consequences for breaching contracts in the films *Bamboozled* (2000) and *X* (1992)? The characters that break their contract are classified into two types of tragic heroes: heroes that experience a higher revelation by breaking their contract, and heroes who feel lost and abandoned. Malcolm X and Cheeba fit into the first type of tragic hero. Both Malcolm and Cheeba break their contract on their own accord. They feel that their life is a statement or a principle. A key component to being the first type of tragic hero is responsibility. Both Malcolm and Cheeba feel that their lives are examples of something much more special than the natural labors and functions of life. Both Malcolm and Cheeba's conversion leads them to a new way of understanding, seeing, thinking, and knowing. Although Cheeba does not die, Malcolm's thinking propels him to his death. But his death is not so straightforward. Malcolm's death is what gives his life meaning; it is a battle against the absurdity of life. It is life.

Implications for the Future

This research made a concerted effort to explore black identity through the films *Bamboozled* (2000) and *X* (1992). Individuals who want to explore Lee's vision of black identity might want to use different films. The researcher believes that Lee's other films, such as Clockers, School Daze, and the Twenty-Fifth Hour, are just as applicable for research. If future researchers are to share Lee's (1992, 2000) vision of black identity, then they might want to use more contemporary films. Arguably, as Lee (1992, 2000) matures, so does his understanding of black identity.

The second point of interest is gender issues. Researchers such as Lucia (2001), McPhail (1996a), Diawara (1993), and Reid (1993) have made remarks concerning Lee's failure to recognize the importance of black women in his films. The researcher believes that an examination of black identity must include vested interest in the scrutiny of black women. Reid (1993) noted that She's Gotta Have It and School Daze present a negative portrait of black women. The female protagonist, Nola Darling, is involved with three lovers. Each of Nola's lovers attempts to coerce her into a monogamous relationship, but she declines. Reid (1993) also reported, "In She's Gotta Have It, it's Jamie's rape of Nola, and in School Daze its...Dap finding out that Julian [Jane's lover] coerced Jane into going to bed with Half Pint" (p. 95). These are just some issues that future researchers can focus on. The recurring theme mentioned in this document is that black identity is heterogeneous and needs to be explored to its fullest, even if that means researchers focus on areas that are historically unpopular.

Researcher's Contribution

This study of *Bamboozled* (2000) and *X* (1992) can serve as a starting point to reexamine black identity and its negotiation. The researcher has applied various concepts and ideas to show the complexity of identity. It is the researcher's hope that this study creates an insurgent curiosity as to dynamic notion of black identity and that film will be one of the tools used to articulate this information. Because black identity is a fluid concept, the researcher hopes this study contributes to the ongoing dynamic. The researcher believes that the fluid-like nature of black metaphor is exciting and provides African Americans with the opportunity to define themselves in a more appropriate fashion.

Given the rhetorical efficacy of film, the researcher hopes that film directors are more cognizant of the films they direct. Bazin (1974) noted that film also has the ability to blur the lines between what is perceivably fact and what is fiction. Since film possesses this rhetorical property, it is incumbent that film directors take heed to the power of this media. The researcher hopes that this document is the starting point.

Glossary

alienation   A black existential term that describes the agony and despair of the modern day African American who has an identity crisis (West, 1993)

blackface   A performance style that usually consisted of several white male performers parodying the songs, dances, and speech patterns of southern blacks. Performers blackened their faces with burnt cork and dressed in rags as they played the banjo, the bone castanets, the fiddle, and the tambourine. In the late 1820s, blackface minstrelsy dominated American popular entertainment (Mahar, 1998).

blaxploitation films   Situated in the late sixties to the early seventies, these films exploited black people, offering a warped view of black culture. In particular, they showcased blacks as hot-tempered and unpredictable. Films such as *Shaft* (1971) and *Superfly* (1972) are examples of blaxploitation (Koven, 2001).

complicity of negative difference   A theory that locates logocentric, xenophobic, and essentialist thinking within discourse (McPhail, 1991)

cultural contract   A theory of identity coined by Ronald Jackson (2002). The cultural contract paradigm suggests that at any given point in time, human beings are coordinating relationships founded upon assimilation, adaptation, or valuation.

double-consciousness   A black existentialist term that specifically speaks to the black identity and cultural awareness that blacks feel in relationship to mainstream society (Du Bois, 1903). Specifically, "double-consciousness" is this sense of one looking at one's self through the eyes of others, of measuring one's soul by the tape of a world that looks on in amused contempt and pity (Dubois, 1903).

essentialism   Describes a "reality in which material and symbolic processes exist in and of themselves, in which they are justified either on the basis of belief in some externally validated, reliably referenced reality [that]…is aimed at the discovery of essential truths" (McPhail, 1996a)

hermeneutical ethos A pragmatic approach to understanding cultural conflict and difference; it measures itself by the degree to which it achieves praxis in real-life situations. Watts (2002) noted that a "hermeneutical ethos" exhibits an aesthetic practice that is sensitive to ways in which one makes the best decision.

identity The rhetorical and the social dimensions of culture and society that are fluctuating. These dimensions influence an individual's identity in communicative interactions (Hall & du Gay, 1996).

negative difference Adherence to a set of ideological restraints and principles that argue an essential reality (McPhail, 1996a)

References

Asante, Molefi. "Intellectual Dislocation: Applying Analytic Afrocentricity to Narratives of Identity." *Howard Journal of Communication* 13 (2002): 97–110.
Asante, Molefi K. *The Afrocentric Idea*. Philadelphia: Temple University Press, 1998.
Baldwin, James. *If Beale Street Could Talk*. New York: The Dial Press, 1974.
Bazin, André. *Renoir*. London: W.H. Allen, 1974.
Bensen, W. Thomas. "Rhetoric and Autobiography: The Case of Malcolm X." *The Quarterly Journal of Speech* 60 (1974): 1–25.
Bosmajian, Haig A. *The Language of Oppression*. Lanham, Md.: University Press of America, 1983.
Breitman, George. *Malcolm X Speaks: Selected Speeches and Statements*. New York: Vintage, 1982.
Burke, Kenneth. *Language as Symbolic Action: Essays on Life, Literature, and Method*. London: University of California, 1966.
Cripps, Thomas. *Slow Fade to Black: The Negro in American Film, 1900–1942*. New York: Oxford University Press, 1977.
Crowdus, Gary, & Dan Georakas. "Thinking About the Power of Images: An Interview with Spike Lee." *Cineaste* 26 (2001): 4–6.
Diawara, Manthia. *Black American Cinema*. New York: Routledge, 1993.
Du Bois, W. E. B. *The Souls of Black Folk*. Chicago: A. C. McClurg, 1903.
Fairclough, Norman. *Looking at Language, Power and Ideology*. New York: Vintage Books, 1992.
Fanon, Frantz. *Black Skin, White Masks*. New York: Grove Press, 1991.
Gill, Ann. *Rhetoric and Human Understanding*. Chicago: Wavelength Press, 1994.
Godfried, Nathan. "Identity, Power and Local Television: African Americans, Organized Labor and UHF-TV in Chicago, 1962–1968." *Historical Journal of Film, Radio and Television* 22 (2002): 117–30.
Hall, Stuart, & Paul du Gay. *Questions of Cultural Identity*. Thousand Oaks, Ca.: Sage Publications, 1996.
Hecht, Michael L., Mary J. Collier, & Sidney Ribeau. "African American Communication: Ethnic Identity and Cultural Interpretation." *Communication Monographs* 66 (1993): 178–97.

References

Jackson, Ronald L. "Exploring African American Identity Negotiation in the Academy: Toward a Transformative Vision of African American Communication Scholarship." *Howard Journal of Communications* 13 (2002): 43–57.

Jackson, Ronald L. *The Negotiation of Cultural Identity: Perceptions of European Americans and African Americans.* Westport, Conn.: Blackwood, 1999.

Koven, J. Mikel. *Blaxploitation Films.* Reading, Berkshire, UK: Cox & Wyman, 2001.

Leader, Edward Roland. *Understanding Malcolm X: The Controversial Changes in His Political Philosophy.* New York: Vantage Press, 1993.

Lee, Spike. *Bamboozled.* Universal City, Ca.: Forty Acres and a Mule, 2000. Film.

Lee, Spike. *X.* Universal City, Ca.: Forty Acres and a Mule, 1992. Film.

Littlejohn, Stephen W. *Theories of Human Communication.* 2d ed. Belmont, Ca.: Wadsworth, 1996.

Llorens, David. *The Fellah, the Chosen Ones. The Guardian in Black Fire.* New York: William Morrow and Company, 1968.

Locke, Alain, ed. *The New Negro: An Interpretation.* New York: Arno Press, 1925.

Lubiano, Wahneema, ed. *The House that Race Built: Black Americans, U.S. Terrain.* New York: Random House, 1998.

Lucia, Cynthia. "Race, Media and Money: A Critical Symposium on Spike Lee's 'Bamboozled.'" *Cineaste* 26 (2001): 10–11.

Mahar, William J. *Behind the Burnt Cork Mask: Early Blackface Minstrelsy and Antebellum American Popular Culture.* Chicago: University of Illinois Press, 1998.

Martin, Judith N., & Thomas K. Nakayama. *Experiencing Intercultural Communication: An Introduction.* New York: McGraw-Hill, 1999.

McKay, Claude. *Home to Harlem.* New York: Harper & Bros., 1928.

McPhail, Mark Lawrence. "Complicity: The Theory of Negative Difference." *Howard Journal of Communication* 3 (1991): 1–13.

McPhail, Mark Lawrence. "Dessentializing Difference: Transformative Visions in Contemporary Black Thought." *Howard University Journal of Communication* 13 (2002): 77–95.

McPhail, Mark Lawrence. "Race and Sex in Black and White: Essence and Ideology in Spike Lee's Discourse." *Howard Journal of Communication* 7 (1996a): 127–38.

McPhail, Mark Lawrence. *The Rhetoric of Racism.* Lanham, Md.: University Press of America, 1994.

McPhail, Mark Lawrence. *Zen in the Art of Rhetoric: An Inquiry into Coherence.* New York: State University, 1996b.

Painter, Norman "Malcolm X across the genres" (motion picture 'X' and book 'The Autobiography of Malcolm X'). *American Historical Review* 98 (1993): 432–40.

Phillips, William H. *Analyzing Films: A Practical Guide.* New York: Holt, Rinehart, and Winston, 1985.

Reid, Mark A. "The Brand X of Post Negritude Frontier." *Film Criticism* 20 (1995): 17–25.
Reid, Mark A. *Redefining Black Film.* Berkeley: University of California Press, 1993.
Rogin, Michael. "Nowhere Left to Stand: The Burnt Cork Roots of Popular Culture." *Cineaste* 26 (2001): 14–15.
Roy, Abhik, & William Starosta. "Hans-George Gadamer, Language, and Intercultural Communication." *Language and Intercultural Communication* 1 (2001): 6–20.
Tate, Greg. "Bamboozled: White Supremacy and a Black Way of Being Human." *Cineaste* 26 (2001): 15–17.
Terrill, E. Robert. "Colonizing the Borderlines: Shifting Circumference in the Rhetoric of Malcolm X." *Quarterly Journal of Speech* 86 (2000): 67–85.
Tondeur, Cristy. "'Bamboozled' by Blackness." *Black Camera,* 16 (2001): 10–11.
Washington, Robert E. *The Ideologies of African American Literature: From the Harlem Renaissance to the Black Nationalist Revolt: A Sociology of Literature Perspective.* Lanham, Md.: Rowman & Littlefield, 2001.
Watts, Eric. "African American Ethos and Hermeneutical Rhetoric: An Exploration of Alain Locke's The New Negro." *Quarterly Journal of Speech* 88 (2002): 1–18.
West, Cornel. *Keeping Faith: Philosophy and Race in America.* New York: Routledge, 1993.
Wilson, H. Kirt. "Towards a Discursive Theory of Racial Identity: The Souls of Blackfolk as a Response to Nineteenth-Century Biological Determinism." *Western Journal of Communication* 68 (1999): 193–215.
Wright, Richard, and F. Hailu. (1989). "Conceptualizing Language as Ideology." *Howard Journal of Communication,* 1, 174–86.
Zahar, Renate. *Colonialism and Alienation: Concerning Frantz Fanon's Political Theory.* Benin City, Nigeria: Ethiope Publishing Corp, 1974.

About the Author

Gerald A. Powell, Jr., Ph.D. is Professor of Rhetoric at Saint Joseph's College, Rensselaer, Indiana. He received his doctorate degree at Howard University in 2003. His works include "'En Soi—Por Soi' Sartrean Implications of an Existential Ethic Within Interpersonal Communication" and "A Rhetoric of Identity: An Inquiry into Symbolic Syntax, and Composition of Identity in *Bamboozled*." Dr. Powell's work in progress is a text titled "Feuillitons and Rhetorical Essays: A Philosophical Investigation." Dr. Powell's research interests are semiotics, interpersonal communication, existential communication, and philosophy.